30 Day Devotional - Bold and Strong- Coffee Devotions for a Courageous Christian Walk

Joshua Rhoades

Published by Joshua Paul Rhoades, 2024.

While every precaution has been taken in the preparation of this book, the publisher assumes no responsibility for errors or omissions, or for damages resulting from the use of the information contained herein.

30 DAY DEVOTIONAL - BOLD AND STRONG- COFFEE DEVOTIONS FOR A COURAGEOUS CHRISTIAN WALK

First edition. July 29, 2024.

Copyright © 2024 Joshua Rhoades.

ISBN: 979-8224425365

Written by Joshua Rhoades.

Also by Joshua Rhoades

Courage Under Fire: David's Stand On The Battlefield
Jonah's Journey: Voices Of Redemption And Lessons In Obedience
The Furnace Of Faith: 12 Principles From The Heat Of Faith
Whispers of Hope: Inspiring Stories of Men's Prayers In Scripture
Frontier Legends: The Oregon Dream
Elijah: A Beacon Of Boldness
HOOK, LINE & SAVIOUR - Faith Reflections from Fishing
Driven By Faith: Motor Racing Inspired Christian Life
30 Day Devotional - Bold and Strong- Coffee Devotions for a
Courageous Christian Walk
Authentic Christianity: The Heart of Old Time Religion
Consider The Ant - God's Tiny Preachers
Flee Fornication: The Plea For Purity
Renewed Hope- How to Find Encouragement in God
Sounding The Call - The Voice of Conviction
The Altar - Where Heaven Meets Earth
The Bible's Battlefields- Timeless Lessons from Ancient Wars
The Sacred Art of Silence - How Silence Speaks in Scripture
Under Fire- The Sanctity of the Traditional Biblical Home
Who Is on the Lord's Side? A Call to Righteousness
What Is Truth? - From Skepticism to Submission
First and Goal- Faith and Football Fundamentals
From Dugout to Devotion- Spiritual Lessons from Baseball
Par for the Course- Faith and Fairways
The Believer's Pace- Tools for Running Life's Marathon

The Immutable Fortress- Security in God's Unchanging Nature
Biblical Bravery

Chapter 1 Espresso (Italy)

"I can do all things through Christ which strengtheneth me." Philippians 4:13

Ingredients:

- 18-20 grams of finely ground coffee beans
- Fresh, filtered water

Equipment:

- Espresso machine

Instructions:

1. Preheat the espresso machine.
2. Fill the portafilter with finely ground coffee, and tamp it down firmly and evenly.
3. Insert the portafilter into the machine and lock it in place.
4. Start the machine, and let the espresso brew for about 2530 seconds, aiming for 1-2 ounces of espresso.
5. Serve immediately in a pre-warmed espresso cup.

Walking courageously with the Lord is much like enjoying a strong espresso. Espresso is concentrated and powerful, providing a quick boost of energy. Similarly, having a strong faith in God can energize and sustain us through life's challenges. When we trust in the Lord, we can face difficulties with confidence, knowing that God is our strength. The Bible tells us in Philippians 4:13, "I can do all things through Christ which strengtheneth me." This verse reminds us that, just as espresso gives us a physical boost, our faith in Christ gives us the spiritual strength to overcome obstacles. A courageous walk with the Lord means believing in His promises and relying on His power, rather than our own.

Imagine a man starting his day with a cup of espresso. The rich, bold flavor awakens his senses and prepares him for the tasks ahead. In the same way, starting our day with prayer and reading the Bible can awaken our spiritual senses and prepare us for the challenges we might face. Faith is not just a passive belief; it is an active, powerful force that can transform our lives. When we have faith, we are not afraid to step out of our comfort zones because we know that God is with us.

A man who walks courageously with the Lord is like a soldier equipped for battle. He knows that his strength comes from God, and this knowledge gives him the courage to face any foe. The Bible is full of stories of men who trusted in God and saw amazing results. Think of David, who faced the giant Goliath with nothing but a sling and a stone, but with great faith in God. His faith was his greatest weapon. Similarly, our faith can help us overcome the "giants" in our lives, whether they are fears, doubts, or challenges.

Walking courageously with the Lord also means being able to stand firm in our beliefs, even when it's not easy. The world may try to sway us or make us doubt, but our faith keeps us grounded. Just as espresso can keep us alert and focused, our faith keeps us spiritually alert and focused on God. When we trust in God's plan, we can remain steadfast, even in the face of adversity.

Having a courageous walk with the Lord also involves sharing our faith with others. Just as we might share a cup of espresso with a friend to give them a boost, we can share our faith to encourage and uplift others. Our testimonies of God's goodness can inspire those around us and help them see the power of faith in action.

Another important aspect of walking courageously with the Lord is recognizing that we are never alone. God is always with us, guiding us and providing the strength we need. This assurance can give us the courage to take on new challenges and pursue our dreams. Knowing that God is by our side makes us bolder and more willing to take risks.

Living a life of courageous faith also means trusting God with our future. We might not always know what lies ahead, but we can be confident that God has a plan for us. This trust allows us to live without fear and anxiety. Just as a strong espresso can wake us up and make us ready for the day, our faith wakes us up spiritually and makes us ready to face whatever comes our way.

Walking courageously with the Lord is a daily commitment. It's about making a conscious decision to trust God in every situation. This means praying regularly, reading the Bible, and surrounding ourselves with other believers who can encourage us. Just as a good espresso is made with quality ingredients, a strong faith is built on a solid foundation of spiritual practices.

In conclusion, walking courageously with the Lord is like enjoying a strong espresso. It gives us the boost we need to face life's challenges with confidence and strength. By trusting in God's promises and relying on His power, we can live boldly and fearlessly. Remember, as Philippians 4:13 says, "I can do all things through Christ which strengtheneth me." This verse is a powerful reminder that with God, all things are possible. So, let's take that courageous walk with the Lord, knowing that He is our strength and our guide.

Chapter 2 Café au Lait (France)

"For as the body without the spirit is dead, so faith without works is dead also." James 2:26

Ingredients:

- 1 cup strong brewed coffee (French press or drip coffee)
- 1 cup steamed milk

Equipment:

- Coffee maker or French press
- Milk steamer or saucepan

Instructions:

1. Brew a strong cup of coffee using a French press or drip coffee maker.
2. Steam the milk until it's hot and frothy. If you don't have a steamer, heat the milk in a saucepan and froth using a whisk or frothing wand.
3. Pour the hot coffee into a large cup or bowl.
4. Add the steamed milk to the coffee, maintaining a ratio of equal parts coffee to milk.
5. Stir gently and serve immediately.

Walking courageously with the Lord is like enjoying a café au lait, a harmonious blend of coffee and milk, symbolizing the perfect balance we need in our lives. A café au lait combines the rich, bold flavor of coffee with the smooth, calming taste of milk, creating a delightful drink that brings comfort and energy. Similarly, our walk with God requires a balance between faith and works, where our belief in God and our actions are in harmony. The Bible teaches us in James 2:26, "For as the body without the spirit is dead, so faith without works is dead also." This verse highlights the importance of having both faith and works in our lives. Just as a café au lait would not be the same without either coffee or milk, our spiritual lives are incomplete without both faith and good deeds.

Imagine starting your day with a cup of café au lait. The warmth and richness of the drink wake you up and prepare you for the day ahead. In the same way, starting our day with prayer and reflection on God's word can energize us spiritually, helping us face whatever challenges come our way. When we blend our faith with good works, we create a life that is pleasing to God and beneficial to those around us. Just as the coffee and milk complement each other in a café au lait, our faith and works should complement each other, working together to reflect God's love and grace.

Walking courageously with the Lord means striving to maintain this balance in every aspect of our lives. It involves trusting God wholeheartedly while also taking action to live out our faith. When we have faith without works, it is like having coffee without milk or milk without coffee – something is missing, and the experience is not complete. Similarly, works without faith are empty and lack the true purpose that comes from a relationship with God. True courage comes from knowing that our faith is not just a belief in our hearts but is also demonstrated through our actions. By living out our faith through good works, we show the world the love and compassion of Christ.

One of the key aspects of a courageous walk with the Lord is recognizing that our actions matter. Every kind deed, every moment of service, every act of love is a reflection of our faith in God. Just as a well-made café au lait requires the right proportions of coffee and milk, our lives require the right balance of faith and works. This balance helps us grow spiritually and makes our faith more robust and meaningful.

It also allows us to be effective witnesses for Christ, showing others the transformative power of God's love through our actions.

In our daily lives, there are countless opportunities to blend our faith with good works. It could be helping a neighbor in need, volunteering at a local shelter, or simply being a source of encouragement to someone going through a tough time. Each of these actions, when done with a heart of faith, strengthens our relationship with God and brings us closer to Him. It is in these moments that we truly understand the meaning of James 2:26. Our faith comes alive through our works, just as the flavors of coffee and milk come alive in a café au lait.

Walking courageously with the Lord also means being intentional about our spiritual growth. This involves spending time in prayer, reading the Bible, and seeking God's guidance in all we do. Just as a café au lait is best enjoyed when the ingredients are of high quality, our spiritual lives flourish when we invest time and effort into nurturing our faith. This intentionality helps us stay grounded in God's word and keeps us focused on His will for our lives. It also empowers us to take bold steps of faith, knowing that our actions are backed by our trust in God.

Another important aspect of a courageous walk with the Lord is the ability to persevere through challenges. Life is not always easy, and there will be times when our faith is tested. In these moments, it is crucial to remember the balance of faith and works. Our faith gives us the strength to endure, while our works provide the means to make a positive impact despite the difficulties. Just as a café au lait can provide comfort and warmth on a cold day, our faith and works can provide the comfort and strength we need to face life's storms.

Furthermore, walking courageously with the Lord means being a light to those around us. Our balanced lives of faith and works can inspire others to seek God and live out their faith in meaningful ways. Just as the aroma of a café au lait can draw people in, the fragrance of our good works can draw others to Christ. By living out our faith authentically and consistently, we become ambassadors of God's love and grace, showing the world the beauty of a life fully surrendered to Him.

In addition, maintaining a balance of faith and works helps us build a strong community of believers. When we work together, supporting and encouraging one another, we create a powerful force for good in the world. Just as a café au lait is enjoyed best in the company of friends, our faith is strengthened in the fellowship of other believers. Together, we can accomplish great things for God's kingdom, each one of us contributing our unique gifts and talents.

Walking courageously with the Lord also involves humility. We must recognize that our good works are not for our glory but for God's. Just as a café au lait is a blend of two distinct ingredients working together, our lives should be a blend of faith and works working together to bring glory to God. This humility keeps us grounded and reminds us that everything we do is by God's grace and for His purposes.

In conclusion, walking courageously with the Lord is like enjoying a well-balanced café au lait. It requires blending our faith with good works, creating a harmonious and fulfilling spiritual life. By maintaining this balance, we can grow closer to God, make a positive impact on those around us, and live out our faith in meaningful ways. Remember, as James 2:26 says, "For as the body without the spirit is dead, so faith without works is dead also." Let us strive to live lives that are a perfect blend of faith and works, bringing glory to God and reflecting His love to the world. Just as a café au lait brings comfort and energy, our balanced lives of faith and works can bring comfort and hope to those in need. So, let us take that courageous walk with the Lord, knowing that He is our strength and our guide, and let our lives be a testament to the powerful blend of faith and works.

Chapter 3 Turkish Coffee (Turkey)

"Study to shew thyself approved unto God, a workman that needeth not to be ashamed, rightly dividing the word of truth." 2 Timothy 2:15
Ingredients:

- 1 cup water
- 1-2 teaspoons finely ground Turkish coffee
- Sugar (optional, to taste)
- Cardamom (optional, for extra flavor)

Equipment:

- Cezve (Turkish coffee pot)
- Small coffee cup

Instructions:

1. Measure the water with the coffee cup and pour it into the cezve.
2. Add the finely ground coffee and sugar (if using) to the cezve.
3. Stir the mixture until the coffee and sugar are dissolved.
4. Place the cezve on low heat and let it slowly come to a boil.
5. As the coffee begins to foam, remove it from the heat just before it overflows.

1. Carefully pour the coffee into the cup, including the foam.
2. Let the grounds settle for a minute before sipping.

Walking courageously with the Lord is much like enjoying a cup of Turkish coffee, which is rich and deep, brewed with care and patience, symbolizing a deep, well-studied faith. Turkish coffee is known for its strong, robust flavor and the meticulous process involved in making it, requiring finely ground coffee beans, water, and sometimes sugar, all brewed slowly to allow the flavors to fully develop. Similarly, a deep and well-studied faith in God requires time, effort, and careful attention. To truly understand the richness of God's word, we must delve deeply into the scriptures, just as the coffee grounds in Turkish coffee are immersed in water, allowing every nuance of flavor to be extracted. The Bible encourages us in 2 Timothy 2:15, "Study to shew thyself approved unto God, a workman that needeth not to be ashamed, rightly dividing the word of truth." This verse highlights the importance of studying God's word diligently, so we can be approved by God and confidently share the truth with others. Just as Turkish coffee is a product of careful brewing and patience, our faith grows stronger and richer when we invest time in studying the Bible, understanding its teachings, and applying them to our lives.

Imagine starting your day with a cup of Turkish coffee, taking the time to appreciate its rich aroma and flavor. In the same way, starting our day with a deep dive into the scriptures can awaken our spiritual senses and prepare us for the challenges ahead. A man who walks courageously with the Lord does not settle for a superficial understanding of the Bible but seeks to understand its depths, allowing the truth of God's word to permeate every aspect of his life. This requires discipline and dedication, much like the process of making Turkish coffee. It involves setting aside time each day to read the Bible, meditate on its meaning, and seek God's guidance in understanding how to apply it to our daily lives.

Walking courageously with the Lord also means being willing to ask questions and seek answers. Just as a coffee connoisseur might explore different brewing methods and coffee varieties to find the perfect cup, a man of faith seeks to understand the different aspects of God's word, asking questions, studying different interpretations, and seeking wisdom from trusted sources. This journey of exploration and discovery helps deepen our faith, as we gain a more comprehensive understanding of who God is and what He desires for our lives. By studying the Bible diligently, we equip ourselves with the knowledge and wisdom needed to navigate life's challenges and make decisions that honor God.

In our daily lives, there are many opportunities to delve deeper into the scriptures and grow in our faith. This could involve participating in a Bible study group, listening to sermons and teachings, or reading books and articles that provide insights into the Bible. Just as a well-made cup of Turkish coffee is the result of careful preparation and attention to detail, a deep and well-studied faith is the result of consistent effort and a desire to know God more intimately. This commitment to studying God's word helps us build a strong foundation for our faith, enabling us to stand firm in our beliefs and face challenges with confidence.

A man who walks courageously with the Lord also recognizes the importance of applying the knowledge gained from studying the Bible to his daily life. Just as Turkish coffee is meant to be savored and enjoyed, the truths we discover in the scriptures are meant to be lived out and shared with others. This means aligning our actions with God's teachings, treating others with love and respect, and making decisions that reflect our commitment to following Christ. By living out our faith in tangible ways, we demonstrate the transformative power of God's word and inspire others to seek a deeper relationship with Him.

Walking courageously with the Lord also involves being open to correction and growth. As we study the Bible, we may encounter passages that challenge our current beliefs or behaviors. Just as a coffee enthusiast might adjust their brewing method to improve the flavor of their coffee, we must be willing to adjust our attitudes and actions to align more closely with God's word. This requires humility and a willingness to submit to God's guidance, recognizing that His wisdom is greater than our own. By being open to correction and growth, we allow God's word to shape and refine us, helping us become more like Christ in our thoughts, words, and actions.

Another important aspect of a courageous walk with the Lord is the ability to share the richness of God's word with others. Just as Turkish coffee is often shared with friends and family, our faith is meant to be shared with those around us. This could involve having conversations about our faith, sharing our personal experiences of God's goodness, or simply living in a way that reflects the love and grace of Christ. By sharing the richness of God's word with others, we help spread the light of the gospel and encourage others to seek a deeper relationship with God.

Walking courageously with the Lord also means trusting in His promises and relying on His strength. Just as Turkish coffee provides a strong, invigorating boost, our faith in God gives us the strength to face life's challenges with courage and confidence. When we trust in God's promises, we can be assured that He will provide for us, guide us, and give us the strength we need to overcome any obstacle. This trust allows us to live boldly and fearlessly, knowing that God is with us every step of the way.

Living a life of courageous faith also means being patient and persistent. Just as Turkish coffee requires time to brew and develop its rich flavor, our faith requires time and persistence to grow and mature. There may be times when we face doubts or challenges, but it is important to remain steadfast in our commitment to studying God's word and seeking His guidance. By persevering in our faith, we allow God to work in us and through us, helping us grow stronger and more resilient.

In conclusion, walking courageously with the Lord is like enjoying a cup of Turkish coffee, rich and deep, brewed with care and patience. It requires a deep and well-studied faith, built on the foundation of God's word. By studying the scriptures diligently, seeking to understand their richness, and applying their truths to our daily lives, we can grow in our faith and walk courageously with the Lord. Just as 2 Timothy 2:15 encourages us to "study to shew thyself approved unto God, a workman that needeth not to be ashamed, rightly dividing the word of truth," let us commit to delving deeply into the scriptures, understanding their richness, and living out their truths in our lives. In doing so, we can experience the fullness of God's love and grace, and inspire others to seek a deeper relationship with Him. So, let us take that courageous walk with the Lord, knowing that He is our strength and our guide, and let our lives be a testament to the richness and depth of a well-studied faith.

Chapter 4 Café Cubano (Cuba)

"The joy of the Lord is your strength." Nehemiah 8:10
Ingredients:

- 1 tablespoon finely ground Cuban coffee (e.g., Bustelo or

Pilon)

- 2 tablespoons sugar

Equipment:

- Espresso machine or stovetop espresso maker
- Small cup or demitasse

Instructions:

1. Brew the coffee using an espresso machine or stovetop espresso maker.
2. Place the sugar in a small cup.
3. As soon as the first few drops of coffee come out, pour them into the sugar and stir vigorously to create a creamy, light brown paste (espuma).
4. Continue brewing the coffee and once it's ready, pour it over the sugar mixture, stirring to combine.
5. Serve immediately in a small cup.

Walking courageously with the Lord is much like savoring a cup of Café Cubano, which is sweet and strong, symbolizing the joy found in faith. Café Cubano, a traditional Cuban coffee, is known for its rich, bold flavor and sweet, frothy top layer created by mixing the first few drops of brewed espresso with sugar. This delightful blend provides an energizing and uplifting experience, much like the joy we experience when we walk closely with God. The Bible tells us in Nehemiah 8:10, "The joy of the Lord is your strength." This verse reminds us that our strength comes from the joy we find in our relationship with God. Just as Café Cubano combines the robust strength of espresso with the sweetness of sugar, our faith combines the strength of God's promises with the sweetness of His love and grace. When we allow the joy of the Lord to fill our hearts, we are empowered to face life's challenges with courage and optimism, and we can sweeten the lives of those around us by sharing this joy.

Imagine starting your day with a cup of Café Cubano. The strong, rich coffee awakens your senses, while the sweetness brings a smile to your face. In the same way, starting our day with prayer and reflection on God's word can fill us with joy and prepare us for whatever lies ahead. A man who walks courageously with the Lord is not just strong in his faith but also joyful. This joy is not dependent on circumstances but is rooted in the assurance of God's love and the hope of His promises. Just as the sugar in Café Cubano enhances the flavor of the coffee, the joy of the Lord enhances our lives, making us more resilient, more compassionate, and more willing to serve others.

Walking courageously with the Lord means letting this joy be evident in all we do. It involves having a positive attitude, even in difficult times, and trusting that God is in control.

Just as the sweet froth on top of a Café Cubano is a visible sign of the sugar mixed in, our joy should be a visible sign of our faith. People around us should be able to see the joy of the Lord in our actions, our words, and our interactions with others. This joy is contagious and can inspire and uplift those who are struggling or feeling down. By sharing the joy of the Lord, we can make a positive impact on the lives of others, just as a good cup of Café Cubano can lift someone's spirits.

In our daily lives, there are many opportunities to share the joy of the Lord with others. It could be through a kind word, a helping hand, or simply a smile. Each of these actions, when done with a heart full of joy, can brighten someone's day and remind them of God's love. Just as Café Cubano is a blend of strong and sweet, our actions should be a blend of strength and kindness. By showing both the strength of our faith and the sweetness of God's love, we can be a powerful witness to the world.

Walking courageously with the Lord also means finding joy in the little things. Life is full of moments that can bring us joy if we take the time to notice them. It could be the beauty of a sunrise, the laughter of a child, or the comfort of a good conversation with a friend. Just as we savor each sip of a wellmade Café Cubano, we should savor these moments of joy and thank God for them. This attitude of gratitude helps us stay positive and focused on the blessings in our lives, even when we face challenges.

Another important aspect of a courageous walk with the Lord is the ability to find joy in serving others. When we use our gifts and talents to help those in need, we not only bless them but also experience the joy of fulfilling God's purpose for our lives. Just as a barista takes pride in crafting the perfect cup of Café Cubano, we can take joy in the work we do for God's kingdom. Whether it's volunteering at a local charity, mentoring a young person, or simply being there for a friend in need, each act of service is an opportunity to share the joy of the Lord.

Walking courageously with the Lord also means trusting Him in all circumstances. Life can be unpredictable, and we may face trials and difficulties that test our faith. However, just as the strength of the coffee in Café Cubano is balanced by the sweetness of the sugar, our strength in difficult times is balanced by the joy we find in the Lord. This joy gives us the resilience to persevere and the hope to keep moving forward. When we trust in God's plan and rely on His strength, we can face any challenge with confidence.

Living a life of courageous faith also means being a source of encouragement to others. Just as Café Cubano can provide a quick pick-me-up, our words and actions can lift the spirits of those around us. We can share the joy of the Lord by offering a listening ear, a word of encouragement, or a prayer.

By being a source of joy and support, we help others experience the love of God and strengthen their faith.

Walking courageously with the Lord also involves being joyful in our worship. Worship is not just a duty but a joyful expression of our love for God. Whether we are singing hymns, praying, or reading the Bible, our worship should be filled with joy and gratitude. Just as the rich, sweet flavor of Café Cubano can make our taste buds dance, the joy of worship can make our spirits soar. When we worship with joy, we draw closer to God and experience His presence in a powerful way.

In conclusion, walking courageously with the Lord is like enjoying a cup of Café Cubano, sweet and strong, filled with the joy of the Lord. By letting this joy be evident in our lives, we can face challenges with strength and optimism, and we can sweeten the lives of those around us. Remember, as

Nehemiah 8:10 says, "The joy of the Lord is your strength." This verse is a powerful reminder that our strength comes from the joy we find in our relationship with God. Just as Café Cubano combines the robust strength of espresso with the sweetness of sugar, our faith combines the strength of God's promises with the sweetness of His love and grace. So, let us walk courageously with the Lord, knowing that His joy is our strength and our guide, and let our lives be a testament to the powerful blend of strength and sweetness found in a deep, joyful faith. By sharing this joy with others, we can make a positive impact on the world and inspire others to seek the joy of the Lord in their own lives. Just as a well-made Café Cubano can lift someone's spirits, our joyful faith can uplift and encourage those around us, making our world a brighter, more hopeful place.

Chapter 5 Café de Olla (Mexico)

"Having then gifts differing according to the grace that is given to us, whether prophecy, let us prophesy according to the proportion of faith." Romans 12:6

Ingredients:

- 4 cups water
- 1/2 cup coarsely ground coffee
- 1 cinnamon stick
- 1/4 cup piloncillo or dark brown sugar
- Optional: orange peel or cloves for additional flavor

Equipment:

- Medium saucepan or traditional Mexican clay pot

Instructions:

1. In a saucepan, bring the water, cinnamon stick, and piloncillo to a boil.
2. Reduce the heat and simmer until the sugar dissolves.
3. Add the coffee grounds and stir to combine.
4. Optional: Add orange peel or cloves for extra flavor.
5. Remove from heat and let it steep for 5 minutes.
6. Strain the coffee through a fine mesh sieve or cheesecloth into cups. 7. Serve hot.

Walking courageously with the Lord can be likened to enjoying a cup of Café de Olla, a traditional Mexican coffee that is rich in flavor and spiced with cinnamon, symbolizing the spice and variety in the Christian life. Café de Olla is unique because it combines coffee with cinnamon and sometimes other spices like cloves and piloncillo, which is an unrefined sugar. This blend of ingredients creates a warm, comforting, and aromatic beverage that is both invigorating and soothing. Similarly, the Christian life is meant to be rich and varied, filled with the unique gifts and flavors that God has given each person. The Bible tells us in Romans 12:6, "Having then gifts differing according to the grace that is given to us, whether prophecy, let us prophesy according to the proportion of faith." This verse reminds us that we all have different gifts and talents, and we are called to use them according to our faith. Just as each ingredient in Café de Olla adds to the overall flavor, each person's unique gifts contribute to the richness of the Christian community.

Imagine starting your day with a cup of Café de Olla. The aroma of cinnamon and coffee fills the air, and the first sip warms you from the inside out. In the same way, embracing the unique gifts and flavors God has given us can fill our lives with warmth and purpose. A man who walks courageously with the Lord recognizes that his gifts are meant to be used for God's glory and the benefit of others. He understands that just as the cinnamon in Café de Olla adds a special touch to the coffee, his unique talents add something special to the body of Christ.

Walking courageously with the Lord involves embracing our individuality and understanding that God has a unique plan for each of us. Just as no two cups of Café de Olla are exactly alike, no two people are exactly the same. We each have our own experiences, perspectives, and gifts that shape who we are and how we can serve God. Embracing our uniqueness allows us to walk boldly in our faith, knowing that God has equipped us with everything we need to fulfill His purpose for our lives.

One important aspect of a courageous walk with the Lord is recognizing and celebrating the diversity within the Christian community. Just as Café de Olla is enhanced by the combination of different spices, the body of Christ is enriched by the diversity of its members. Each person's unique gifts and talents bring something valuable to the table, and when we work together, we create a beautiful and harmonious community. This unity in diversity reflects God's creativity and love for His creation.

Walking courageously with the Lord also means being willing to step out of our comfort zones and use our gifts in new and creative ways. Just as a traditional recipe like Café de Olla can be adapted and personalized, our faith journey can take us in unexpected directions. We might discover new talents or passions that we didn't know we had, and we can use these gifts to serve God and others. This willingness to explore and grow in our faith requires courage and trust in God's guidance.

In our daily lives, there are countless opportunities to use our gifts to bless others. It could be through acts of service, sharing our knowledge and skills, or simply offering a listening ear and a kind word. Each of these actions, when done with a heart full of faith, reflects the love and grace of God. Just as a well-made cup of Café de Olla brings comfort and joy, our actions can bring comfort and joy to those around us.

Walking courageously with the Lord also means being open to learning from others and appreciating their gifts. Just as we might appreciate the different flavors in a cup of Café de Olla, we should appreciate the different strengths and talents of those around us. This attitude of gratitude and respect helps build a strong and supportive community where everyone feels valued and encouraged to contribute.

Another important aspect of a courageous walk with the Lord is the ability to find joy and fulfillment in using our gifts. When we use our talents to serve God, we experience a sense of purpose and satisfaction that comes from knowing we are doing what we were created to do. Just as the flavors in Café de Olla blend together to create a delicious drink, our gifts, when used in harmony with God's will, create a fulfilling and meaningful life.

Walking courageously with the Lord also involves being a good steward of our gifts. We are called to develop and refine our talents, just as a skilled barista perfects the art of making Café de Olla. This means investing time and effort into honing our skills, seeking opportunities to grow, and being willing to take risks and try new things. By being good stewards of our gifts, we honor God and make the most of the opportunities He gives us.

Living a life of courageous faith also means being willing to share our gifts with others, even when it is challenging. Just as the spices in Café de Olla can be bold and assertive, our faith sometimes requires us to step out boldly and share God's love in difficult situations. This might involve standing up for what is right, offering support to someone in need, or simply being a beacon of hope and encouragement in a dark world. By sharing our gifts with courage and compassion, we can make a positive impact on the lives of others and bring glory to God.

Walking courageously with the Lord also means trusting in His plan for our lives. Just as a perfectly brewed cup of Café de Olla requires the right balance of ingredients and careful preparation, our lives require the right balance of faith, trust, and action. When we trust in God's plan, we can navigate the ups and downs of life with confidence, knowing that He is in control and has a purpose for everything we experience. This trust allows us to face challenges with resilience and hope, knowing that God is working all things for our good.

In conclusion, walking courageously with the Lord is like enjoying a cup of Café de Olla, flavored with cinnamon and full of rich, comforting goodness. It involves embracing the unique gifts and flavors God has given each of us and using them to serve Him and others. By celebrating our individuality, appreciating the diversity within the Christian community, and being good stewards of our talents, we can walk boldly in our faith and make a positive impact on the world. Remember, as Romans 12:6 says, "Having then gifts differing according to the grace that is given to us, whether prophecy, let us prophesy according to the proportion of faith." This verse is a powerful reminder that our gifts are a reflection of God's grace, and we are called to use them in a way that honors Him. So, let us take that courageous walk with the Lord, knowing that He has equipped us with everything we need to fulfill His purpose for our lives, and let our lives be a testament to the rich, varied, and beautiful tapestry of God's creation. Just as a well-made cup of Café de Olla can warm the heart and soul, our faithful use of God's gifts can bring warmth, comfort, and joy to those around us, making our world a better and brighter place.

Chapter 6 Café Touba (Senegal)

"For we are unto God a sweet savour of Christ, in them that are saved, and in them that perish." (2 Corinthians 2:15)

Ingredients:

- 1 cup water
- 1 tablespoon finely ground coffee
- 1/4 teaspoon ground Guinea pepper (djar)
- Sugar (optional, to taste)

Equipment:

- Small saucepan
- Coffee filter or fine mesh sieve

Instructions:

1. In a small saucepan, bring the water to a boil.
2. Add the ground coffee and Guinea pepper to the boiling water.
3. Reduce the heat and simmer for about 5 minutes.
4. Remove from heat and let it steep for another 5 minutes.
5. Strain the coffee through a filter or sieve into a cup.
6. Add sugar to taste, if desired.
7. Serve hot.

Walking courageously with the Lord is much like savoring a cup of Café Touba, a traditional Senegalese coffee that is spiced and aromatic, symbolizing the fragrance of a faithful life. Café Touba is unique because it combines coffee with Guinea pepper (djar) and cloves, creating a bold, distinctive flavor and a rich aroma that fills the air. This special blend not only awakens the senses but also symbolizes how our lives, when filled with faith, righteousness, and good deeds, can be a pleasing aroma to God and to those around us. The Bible tells us in 2 Corinthians 2:15, "For we are unto God a sweet savour of Christ, in them that are saved, and in them that perish." This verse reminds us that our lives should emit the sweet fragrance of Christ, reflecting His love, grace, and righteousness in all we do. Just as the spices in Café Touba enhance its flavor and aroma, our good deeds and faithful living enhance our witness for Christ, making our lives a testament to His goodness and transforming power.

Imagine starting your day with a cup of Café Touba. The warm, spiced aroma fills your home, and the first sip is a delightful blend of flavors that invigorate your spirit. In the same way, starting our day with prayer and reflection on God's word can fill our hearts with His presence and prepare us for the day ahead. A man who walks courageously with the Lord lives a life that is not only strong in faith but also rich in good deeds and righteousness. This kind of life is like a pleasing aroma that draws others to God, inspiring them to seek Him and experience His love.

Walking courageously with the Lord means being intentional about filling our lives with the fragrance of Christ. This involves living out our faith in tangible ways, through acts of kindness, compassion, and integrity. Just as the spices in Café Touba are carefully chosen and blended to create a unique flavor, our actions and attitudes should be chosen to reflect Christ's love and righteousness. Every kind word, every act of service, and every moment of integrity adds to the pleasing aroma of our lives, making us effective witnesses for Christ.

In our daily lives, there are countless opportunities to let the fragrance of our faith shine through. It could be through helping a neighbor, volunteering at a local charity, or simply being a source of encouragement to someone who is struggling. Each of these actions, when done with a heart full of faith, reflects the love and grace of God. Just as a wellmade cup of Café Touba brings comfort and warmth, our lives can bring comfort and hope to those around us when we live out our faith with authenticity and love.

Walking courageously with the Lord also means being mindful of how our actions affect others. Just as the aroma of Café Touba can fill a room and uplift those who smell it, our lives should positively impact those around us. This requires us to be intentional about our choices and to strive for excellence in all we do. Whether we are at work, at home, or in our communities, we should aim to reflect the character of Christ in every situation. This kind of intentional living not only honors God but also draws others to Him.

Another important aspect of a courageous walk with the Lord is the willingness to stand out and be different. Just as Café Touba stands out because of its unique blend of spices, our lives should stand out because of our commitment to Christ and our distinctive way of living. This might mean making choices that are counter-cultural or taking a stand for what is right, even when it is not popular. By living according to God's principles and being willing to be different, we set an example for others and demonstrate the transformative power of faith.

Walking courageously with the Lord also involves being a source of encouragement and support to others. Just as the spices in Café Touba add warmth and depth to the coffee, our words and actions can add warmth and depth to the lives of those around us. We can offer a listening ear, a word of encouragement, or a helping hand to someone in need. By being a source of support and encouragement, we reflect the love of Christ and help others experience His grace and kindness.

Living a life of courageous faith also means being consistent in our walk with God. Just as the process of making Café Touba requires consistency and attention to detail, our spiritual lives require consistency in prayer, Bible study, and worship. This consistency helps us stay grounded in our faith and ensures that our lives continue to reflect the fragrance of Christ. By making a habit of seeking God and aligning our actions with His will, we grow stronger in our faith and become more effective witnesses for Him.

Walking courageously with the Lord also means being grateful for the unique blend of gifts and experiences He has given us. Just as each ingredient in Café Touba contributes to its unique flavor, each of our gifts and experiences contributes to who we are and how we can serve God. Embracing our individuality and using our gifts for God's glory allows us to live fulfilling and impactful lives. By recognizing and appreciating the unique ways God has equipped us, we can make the most of every opportunity to serve Him and others.

In conclusion, walking courageously with the Lord is like enjoying a cup of Café Touba, spiced and aromatic, filled with the rich fragrance of a faithful life. It involves living out our faith in tangible ways, being intentional about our actions, and striving to reflect the character of Christ in all we do. By letting our lives be a pleasing aroma to God, filled with righteousness and good deeds, we can be effective witnesses for Christ and make a positive impact on the world around us. Remember, as 2 Corinthians 2:15 says, "For we are unto God a sweet savour of Christ, in them that are saved, and in them that perish." This verse is a powerful reminder that our lives should emit the sweet fragrance of Christ, drawing others to Him and reflecting His love and grace. So, let us take that courageous walk with the Lord, knowing that He is our strength and our guide, and let our lives be a testament to the rich, varied, and beautiful aroma of a faithful life. Just as a well-made cup of Café Touba can warm the heart and soul, our faithful living can bring warmth, comfort, and joy to those around us, making our world a better and brighter place.

Chapter 7 Vietnamese Coffee (Vietnam)

"But let patience have her perfect work, that ye may be perfect and entire, wanting nothing." James 1:4

Ingredients:

- 2 tablespoons coarse ground Vietnamese coffee (e.g., Trung Nguyen)

- 2 tablespoons sweetened condensed milk
- 1 cup hot water

Equipment:

- Vietnamese coffee filter (phin)
- Glass or mug

Instructions:

1. Add the sweetened condensed milk to the bottom of the glass.
2. Place the coffee filter on top of the glass.
3. Add the ground coffee to the filter, and gently press down with the filter's press.
4. Pour a small amount of hot water into the filter to bloom the coffee grounds, then wait 20-30 seconds.
5. Fill the filter with the remaining hot water and let it drip slowly into the glass.
6. Once the dripping stops, stir the coffee and condensed milk together.
7. Serve hot or over ice.

Walking courageously with the Lord can be likened to savoring a cup of Vietnamese coffee, which is unique and distinctive, brewed slowly to develop its rich and flavorful taste. Vietnamese coffee is prepared using a drip filter, allowing hot water to slowly pass through finely ground coffee into a cup containing sweetened condensed milk. This process, which takes time and patience, results in a delicious and aromatic beverage that is enjoyed slowly and thoughtfully. Similarly, our walk with the Lord requires patience and trust in God's timing as we allow our faith to grow gradually. The Bible encourages us in James 1:4, "But let patience have her perfect work, that ye may be perfect and entire, wanting nothing." This verse reminds us that patience is essential for our spiritual growth, helping us become complete and mature in our faith. Just as Vietnamese coffee is brewed slowly to bring out its full flavor, our faith matures over time as we patiently trust in God's plan and timing.

Imagine preparing a cup of Vietnamese coffee. The process requires patience as you wait for the water to drip through the filter, mixing with the coffee grounds to create a rich, strong brew that blends perfectly with the sweetened condensed milk at the bottom. In the same way, developing a deep and resilient faith requires time, patience, and trust in

God. A man who walks courageously with the Lord understands that spiritual growth does not happen overnight. It involves daily commitment to prayer, studying God's word, and living out His teachings. This slow and steady approach allows our faith to develop naturally and robustly, just like the rich flavor of Vietnamese coffee.

Walking courageously with the Lord means embracing the process of growth and transformation, even when it seems slow or challenging. Just as the drip filter in Vietnamese coffee carefully regulates the flow of water, God carefully guides our spiritual journey, allowing us to grow at the right pace. This process requires us to be patient and to trust that God knows what is best for us. We might not always see immediate results, but we can be confident that God is at work in our lives, shaping us into the people He wants us to be.

In our daily lives, there are many opportunities to practice patience and trust in God's timing. It could be waiting for a prayer to be answered, enduring a difficult season, or working towards a long-term goal. Each of these experiences, when faced with patience and faith, helps to strengthen our relationship with God. Just as the slow brewing process of Vietnamese coffee results in a rich and satisfying drink, the process of waiting and trusting in God results in a faith that is strong and resilient.

Walking courageously with the Lord also means being patient with ourselves and others. Spiritual growth is a journey, and we all progress at different rates. Just as it takes time for Vietnamese coffee to brew, it takes time for us to grow in our faith and for others to grow in theirs. This requires us to be compassionate and understanding, offering encouragement and support rather than judgment. By being patient with ourselves and others, we create an environment where everyone can thrive and grow in their relationship with God.

Another important aspect of a courageous walk with the Lord is the willingness to endure challenges and setbacks with patience. Life is full of unexpected twists and turns, and our faith will be tested. Just as the process of brewing Vietnamese coffee requires a steady and consistent flow of water, our faith requires steady and consistent trust in God, even when things are difficult. By enduring challenges with patience, we build a faith that is resilient and unwavering.

Walking courageously with the Lord also means finding joy in the journey, not just the destination. Just as the process of making and enjoying Vietnamese coffee is an experience to be savored, our walk with God is meant to be enjoyed and appreciated. This involves taking time to notice the small blessings, to celebrate progress, and to thank God for His faithfulness. By finding joy in the journey, we cultivate a positive and hopeful attitude, even in the midst of challenges.

Living a life of courageous faith also means being open to God's timing and plan, even when it differs from our own. We might have our own ideas about how our lives should unfold, but God knows what is best for us. Just as the slow brewing process of Vietnamese coffee allows the flavors to develop fully, God's timing allows His plans for our lives to unfold perfectly. Trusting in God's timing requires humility and a willingness to surrender our own plans to Him. By doing so, we experience the fullness of His blessings and the richness of His grace.

Walking courageously with the Lord also involves being patient in our relationships. Just as Vietnamese coffee is often enjoyed with friends and family, our faith is meant to be shared and experienced in community. This requires us to be patient and loving with those around us, recognizing that everyone is on their own spiritual journey. By showing patience and understanding, we build strong and supportive relationships that reflect God's love and grace.

In conclusion, walking courageously with the Lord is like enjoying a cup of Vietnamese coffee, unique and distinctive, brewed slowly to perfection. It requires patience and trust in God's timing as we allow our faith to grow gradually. By embracing the process of spiritual growth, being patient with ourselves and others, and finding joy in the journey, we develop a faith that is strong and resilient. Remember, as James 1:4 says, "But let patience have her perfect work, that ye may be perfect and entire, wanting nothing." This verse is a powerful reminder that patience is essential for our spiritual growth, helping us become complete and mature in our faith. So, let us take that courageous walk with the Lord, knowing that He is our strength and our guide, and let our lives be a testament to the richness and depth of a faith that is patiently and faithfully grown. Just as a well-made cup of Vietnamese coffee can be a delight to the senses, our faithful and patient walk with God can bring delight, hope, and inspiration to those around us, making our world a better and brighter place.

Chapter 8 Flat White (Australia/New Zealand)

"Therefore, my beloved brethren, be ye stedfast, unmoveable, always abounding in the work of the Lord." 1

Corinthians 15:58

Ingredients:

- 1 shot (1.5 oz) espresso
- 2/3 cup steamed milk

Equipment:

- Espresso machine
- Milk steamer

Instructions:

1. Brew a shot of espresso and pour it into a cup.
2. Steam the milk until it's hot and has a velvety microfoam.
3. Pour the steamed milk over the espresso, aiming for a creamy consistency with little foam on top.
4. Serve immediately.

Walking courageously with the Lord can be compared to enjoying a Flat White, a coffee known for its smooth and consistent texture, symbolizing steadfast faith. A Flat White, originating from Australia and New Zealand, is made with a shot of espresso and steamed milk, creating a velvety, smooth beverage that is both comforting and invigorating. This coffee's consistency and smoothness are reminiscent of a faith that remains steadfast and unwavering, regardless of circumstances. The Bible encourages us in 1 Corinthians 15:58,

"Therefore, my beloved brethren, be ye stedfast, unmoveable, always abounding in the work of the Lord." This verse reminds us that our faith should be firm and constant, much like the reliable and smooth experience of a Flat White. A man who walks courageously with the Lord maintains his faith through all of life's ups and downs, trusting in God's unchanging nature and His promises.

Imagine starting your day with a Flat White. The rich, smooth coffee soothes your senses and prepares you for whatever lies ahead. In the same way, starting our day with prayer and reflection on God's word can ground us in our faith, providing the consistency and strength we need to face challenges. A man who walks courageously with the Lord is like a well-made Flat White – consistent, smooth, and unwavering. This kind of faith is not swayed by the trials and tribulations of life but remains firm in the knowledge that God is in control.

Walking courageously with the Lord involves maintaining a consistent relationship with Him, regardless of our circumstances. Just as a Flat White requires the right balance of espresso and steamed milk to achieve its smooth texture, our faith requires a balance of prayer, reading the Bible, and living out God's teachings. This consistency in our spiritual practices helps us stay connected to God and grounded in His truth. When we make it a habit to seek God daily, our faith becomes a steady and reliable source of strength, much like the consistent quality of a Flat White.

In our daily lives, there are many opportunities to practice steadfast faith. It could be through staying committed to our spiritual disciplines, keeping our word, or remaining faithful in our relationships and responsibilities. Each of these actions, when done with a heart full of faith, reflects our trust in God. Just as the smooth texture of a Flat White is achieved through careful preparation, our steadfast faith is developed through consistent effort and reliance on God. By being steadfast in our faith, we become a beacon of stability and hope for those around us, demonstrating the reliability and faithfulness of God.

Walking courageously with the Lord also means being unwavering in our commitment to His work. Just as the Flat White remains smooth and consistent, our dedication to serving God and others should be steadfast and unchanging. This involves being faithful in our service, using our gifts and talents to further God's kingdom, and continuously seeking ways to make a positive impact. By remaining steadfast in our commitment to God's work, we reflect His unchanging love and grace to the world.

Another important aspect of a courageous walk with the Lord is the ability to stand firm in our beliefs, even when faced with opposition or difficulty. Just as a Flat White maintains its smooth consistency, our faith should remain firm and unshaken, even in the face of challenges. This requires us to be deeply rooted in God's word and to trust in His promises. When we stand firm in our faith, we are able to navigate life's storms with confidence, knowing that God is with us and will see us through.

Walking courageously with the Lord also involves being a source of encouragement and support to others. Just as a Flat White can provide comfort and enjoyment, our steadfast faith can provide comfort and encouragement to those around us. We can offer a listening ear, a word of encouragement, or practical help to those in need. By being a source of support and encouragement, we reflect the love of Christ and help others experience His peace and stability.

Living a life of courageous faith also means being consistent in our character and actions. Just as a Flat White is known for its smooth and consistent texture, our lives should be marked by integrity, honesty, and faithfulness. This consistency in our character reflects our commitment to God and His principles. By living with integrity and faithfulness, we build trust and credibility with others, making our witness for Christ more effective.

Walking courageously with the Lord also means trusting in His timing and plan. Just as the process of making a Flat White requires patience and careful attention, our spiritual journey requires us to trust in God's timing and to be patient in the process. This trust allows us to remain steadfast and hopeful, even when things do not go as we planned. By trusting in God's plan, we can face the future with confidence and peace, knowing that He is in control and that His plans for us are good.

In conclusion, walking courageously with the Lord is like enjoying a Flat White, smooth and consistent, symbolizing steadfast faith. It involves maintaining a consistent relationship with God, staying committed to His work, standing firm in our beliefs, and being a source of encouragement to others. By being steadfast in our faith, we reflect the unchanging nature of God and provide a stable and reliable witness to the world. Remember, as 1 Corinthians 15:58 says, "Therefore, my beloved brethren, be ye stedfast, unmoveable, always abounding in the work of the Lord." This verse is a powerful reminder that our faith should be firm and unwavering, much like the consistent quality of a Flat White. So, let us take that courageous walk with the Lord, knowing that He is our strength and our guide, and let our lives be a testament to the steadfast and unchanging nature of our faith. Just as a well-made Flat White can provide comfort and enjoyment, our faithful and consistent walk with God can bring comfort, hope, and inspiration to those around us, making our world a better and brighter place.

Chapter 9 Ethiopian Coffee (Ethiopia)

"Not forsaking the assembling of ourselves together, as the manner of some is; but exhorting one another." (Hebrews

10:25)

Ingredients:

- 1 cup green coffee beans
- 3 cups water
- Optional: spices like cardamom, cloves, or cinnamon

Equipment:

- Ethiopian coffee pot (jebena)
- Mortar and pestle or coffee grinder

Instructions:

1. Roast the green coffee beans in a pan over medium heat until they are dark and fragrant.
2. Grind the roasted beans using a mortar and pestle or coffee grinder.
3. Add water to the jebena and bring to a boil.
4. Add the ground coffee to the boiling water.
5. Optional: Add spices for extra flavor.
6. Let the coffee boil for a few minutes, then remove from heat.
7. Allow the grounds to settle before pouring the coffee into small cups.
8. Serve traditionally with popcorn or bread.

Walking courageously with the Lord can be compared to enjoying Ethiopian coffee, which is traditionally shared in a communal ceremony, symbolizing the importance of fellowship and community. Ethiopian coffee ceremonies are rich in tradition and culture, bringing people together to share in the experience of brewing and drinking coffee. This communal aspect of Ethiopian coffee highlights the significance of gathering together, fostering relationships, and building a sense of community. The Bible encourages us in Hebrews 10:25, "Not forsaking the assembling of ourselves together, as the manner of some is; but exhorting one another." This verse reminds us of the importance of not neglecting to meet together but instead encouraging one another. Just as the Ethiopian coffee ceremony brings people together, our walk with the Lord should involve fostering fellowship and community among believers. A man who walks courageously with the Lord understands the value of gathering with others, sharing in their joys and struggles, and encouraging one another in faith.

Imagine being part of an Ethiopian coffee ceremony. The process is slow and deliberate, with each step carefully taken to ensure the best possible experience. In the same way, building and maintaining a strong community of believers requires time, effort, and intentionality. It involves being present for one another, listening, sharing, and supporting each other through life's challenges. Just as the rich aroma of Ethiopian coffee fills the air and draws people together, our faith and love for one another should create an inviting and supportive environment where everyone feels welcome and valued.

Walking courageously with the Lord means recognizing that we are not meant to walk alone. Just as the Ethiopian coffee ceremony is a communal experience, our spiritual journey is meant to be shared with others. This involves being an active participant in a community of believers, attending church, joining small groups, and finding ways to connect with others who share our faith. By doing so, we can build strong, supportive relationships that help us grow in our faith and encourage us to live out our beliefs in our daily lives.

Fostering fellowship and community among believers also means being willing to invest in others. Just as the preparation of Ethiopian coffee requires time and care, building meaningful relationships requires effort and intentionality. This might involve reaching out to someone who is new to the community, offering to pray with a friend who is going through a difficult time, or simply being available to listen and offer support. By investing in others, we demonstrate the love of Christ and help to create a strong, supportive community where everyone feels valued and cared for.

Walking courageously with the Lord also means being willing to share our lives with others, including our struggles and triumphs. Just as the Ethiopian coffee ceremony is an opportunity to share stories and experiences, our fellowship with other believers should involve openness and vulnerability. This allows us to support one another more effectively and to grow together in our faith. When we share our struggles, we can receive encouragement and prayer from others, and when we share our triumphs, we can celebrate together and give thanks to God.

Another important aspect of a courageous walk with the Lord is the willingness to encourage and exhort one another. Just as the communal aspect of Ethiopian coffee brings people together for mutual support, our fellowship with other believers should involve encouraging one another in our faith. This might involve offering a word of encouragement, sharing a scripture that has been meaningful to us, or simply being a positive presence in someone's life. By encouraging one another, we help to build a strong, supportive community where everyone is inspired to grow in their faith and to live out their beliefs.

Walking courageously with the Lord also means being willing to serve others. Just as the Ethiopian coffee ceremony involves serving coffee to one another, our fellowship with other believers should involve acts of service. This might involve helping someone in need, volunteering our time and talents, or simply offering to help with a task or project. By serving others, we demonstrate the love of Christ and help to build a strong, supportive community where everyone feels valued and cared for.

Living a life of courageous faith also means being willing to forgive and seek reconciliation. Just as the Ethiopian coffee ceremony is an opportunity for people to come together and build relationships, our fellowship with other believers should involve a commitment to forgiveness and reconciliation. This means being willing to forgive those who have wronged us and to seek forgiveness when we have wronged others. By doing so, we help to create a strong, supportive community where everyone feels valued and cared for.

Walking courageously with the Lord also means being willing to grow and learn together. Just as the Ethiopian coffee ceremony is an opportunity to learn about the traditions and culture of Ethiopia, our fellowship with other believers should involve a commitment to learning and growing together in our faith. This might involve attending Bible studies, participating in small groups, or simply having conversations about our faith and beliefs. By learning and growing together, we help to build a strong, supportive community where everyone is inspired to grow in their faith and to live out their beliefs.

In conclusion, walking courageously with the Lord is like enjoying Ethiopian coffee, traditionally shared in a communal ceremony, symbolizing the importance of fellowship and community. It involves recognizing the value of gathering with others, investing in relationships, and encouraging one another in our faith. By fostering fellowship and community among believers, we build strong, supportive relationships that help us grow in our faith and encourage us to live out our beliefs in our daily lives. Remember, as Hebrews 10:25 says, "Not forsaking the assembling of ourselves together, as the manner of some is; but exhorting one another." This verse is a powerful reminder of the importance of not neglecting to meet together but instead encouraging one another. So, let us take that courageous walk with the Lord, knowing that He is our strength and our guide, and let our lives be a testament to the importance of fellowship and community. Just as the Ethiopian coffee ceremony brings people together, our fellowship with other believers should create a strong, supportive community where everyone feels valued and cared for, making our world a better and brighter place.

Chapter 10 Kopi Luwak (Indonesia)

"For where your treasure is, there will your heart be also."
Matthew 6:21

Ingredients:

- 2 tablespoons Kopi Luwak coffee beans
- 1 cup hot water

Equipment:

- Coffee grinder
- French press or drip coffee maker

Instructions:

1. Grind the Kopi Luwak beans to a medium-coarse consistency.
2. Add the ground coffee to the French press or coffee maker.
3. Pour hot water over the coffee grounds.
4. Let it steep for 4 minutes if using a French press, then press the plunger down slowly.
5. Pour the coffee into a cup and serve immediately.

Walking courageously with the Lord can be likened to savoring a cup of Kopi Luwak, which is a rare and expensive coffee from Indonesia, symbolizing the preciousness of faith. Kopi Luwak is known for its unique processing method, where the coffee cherries are eaten by civet cats, fermented in their digestive system, and then harvested from their droppings before being cleaned and roasted. This intricate process makes Kopi Luwak one of the most sought-after and costly coffees in the world. Similarly, our faith is precious and valuable, something that must be cherished and protected. The Bible tells us in Matthew 6:21,

"For where your treasure is, there will your heart be also." This verse reminds us that our hearts are closely tied to what we value most, and if we truly treasure our faith, we will guard it carefully and ensure it remains pure and undefiled. Just as Kopi Luwak is treated with great care and reverence due to its value, our faith deserves the same level of attention and protection.

Imagine starting your day with a cup of Kopi Luwak. The anticipation of tasting such a rare and valuable coffee fills you with excitement. The rich aroma and complex flavors are a reward for the patience and effort invested in obtaining it. In the same way, our faith, which is far more valuable than any earthly treasure, should fill us with a sense of gratitude and awe. A man who walks courageously with the Lord understands the worth of his faith and takes deliberate steps to nurture and protect it. This involves spending time in prayer, reading the Bible, and living according to God's principles. Just as the unique process of making Kopi Luwak requires careful attention, our spiritual growth requires dedication and vigilance.

Walking courageously with the Lord means recognizing the value of our faith and treating it as the precious treasure it is.

This involves being mindful of influences that could defile or diminish our faith. Just as Kopi Luwak must be handled with care to preserve its quality, we must guard our hearts and minds against anything that could corrupt our faith. This might involve avoiding negative influences, resisting temptations, and making choices that align with our beliefs. By doing so, we ensure that our faith remains strong and pure, allowing us to walk boldly and confidently with the Lord.

In our daily lives, there are many opportunities to protect and nurture our faith. It could be through regular church attendance, participating in small groups, or seeking out mentors who can provide guidance and support. Each of these actions, when done with a heart full of faith, helps to strengthen our relationship with God and keep our faith intact. Just as a well-prepared cup of Kopi Luwak brings out the best flavors, our consistent efforts to grow and protect our faith bring out the best in our spiritual lives.

Walking courageously with the Lord also means being willing to invest in our faith. Just as Kopi Luwak is rare and expensive, valuable faith requires investment. This might involve dedicating time each day to prayer and Bible study, seeking out resources that help us grow in our understanding of God's word, or investing in relationships that encourage us in our walk with God. By prioritizing our faith and making it a central part of our lives, we show that we truly value it and are committed to nurturing it.

Another important aspect of a courageous walk with the Lord is the willingness to sacrifice for our faith. Just as Kopi Luwak involves a unique and sometimes difficult process to produce, our faith journey may require us to make sacrifices and endure challenges. This could involve giving up certain habits, making difficult choices, or standing firm in our beliefs even when it is unpopular. By being willing to make these sacrifices, we demonstrate the depth of our commitment to God and the value we place on our faith.

Walking courageously with the Lord also means being a good steward of the faith we have been given. Just as the producers of Kopi Luwak take great care to ensure the quality of their product, we must take great care to live out our faith in a way that honors God. This involves using our gifts and talents to serve others, sharing the gospel with those around us, and living a life that reflects the love and grace of Christ. By being good stewards of our faith, we not only honor God but also inspire others to seek Him.

Living a life of courageous faith also means being open to growth and transformation. Just as the process of making Kopi Luwak involves a transformation from coffee cherry to finished product, our faith journey involves continuous growth and change. This requires us to be open to God's leading, willing to learn and grow, and ready to embrace the new things He wants to do in our lives. By being open to transformation, we allow God to mold us into the people He wants us to be and to use us for His purposes.

Walking courageously with the Lord also means finding joy and fulfillment in our faith. Just as the experience of enjoying a cup of Kopi Luwak is a unique and pleasurable one, our relationship with God should bring us deep joy and satisfaction. This involves taking time to appreciate the blessings in our lives, celebrating the victories, and finding contentment in our walk with God. By finding joy in our faith, we cultivate a positive and hopeful attitude that sustains us through life's challenges.

In conclusion, walking courageously with the Lord is like savoring a cup of Kopi Luwak, rare and expensive, symbolizing the preciousness of faith. It involves recognizing the value of our faith, protecting it from anything that might defile it, and nurturing it with care and dedication. By valuing our faith highly and making it a central part of our lives, we demonstrate our commitment to God and our desire to grow in our relationship with Him. Remember, as Matthew 6:21 says, "For where your treasure is, there will your heart be also." This verse is a powerful reminder that our hearts are closely tied to what we value most, and if we truly treasure our faith, we will guard it carefully and ensure it remains pure and undefiled. So, let us take that courageous walk with the Lord, knowing that He is our strength and our guide, and let our lives be a testament to the preciousness and value of a faith that is nurtured and protected. Just as a well-prepared cup of Kopi Luwak brings out the best flavors, our faithful and dedicated walk with God can bring out the best in our lives, making our world a better and brighter place.

Chapter 11 Café Bombón (Spain)

"O taste and see that the Lord is good: blessed is the man that trusteth in him." Psalm 34:8

Ingredients:

- 1 shot (1.5 oz) espresso
- 1.5 oz sweetened condensed milk

Equipment:

- Espresso machine
- Glass or transparent mug

Instructions:

1. Brew a shot of espresso and set aside.
2. Pour the sweetened condensed milk into the bottom of the glass.
3. Slowly pour the espresso over the condensed milk to create two distinct layers.
4. Serve without stirring to maintain the layers.

Walking courageously with the Lord can be compared to savoring a cup of Café Bombón, a delightful Spanish coffee that combines the rich bitterness of espresso with the sweet creaminess of condensed milk, symbolizing the sweetness of God's promises. Café Bombón is known for its beautiful layers and its dessert-like taste, providing a moment of joy and indulgence in each sip. Similarly, our walk with the Lord should be marked by the delight we take in His promises and the joy we find in His presence. The Bible tells us in Psalm 34:8, "O taste and see that the Lord is good: blessed is the man that trusteth in him." This verse invites us to experience the goodness of God, much like savoring the sweet and rich flavors of Café Bombón, and to find our blessings in trusting Him. Just as Café Bombón is a treat that brings a smile to our faces, God's promises are sweet and delightful, offering us hope, joy, and encouragement in our journey of faith.

Imagine starting your day with a cup of Café Bombón. The process of making it involves carefully layering espresso and sweetened condensed milk, resulting in a drink that is visually appealing and wonderfully delicious. In the same way, starting our day by reflecting on God's promises can fill our hearts with joy and set a positive tone for the day ahead. A man who walks courageously with the Lord finds joy in God's promises and lets that joy radiate to others. This kind of faith is not only about enduring hardships but also about celebrating the goodness and faithfulness of God.

Walking courageously with the Lord means taking delight in His promises and sharing that delight with others. Just as Café Bombón is a blend of flavors that creates a delightful experience, our faith should be a blend of trust in God's promises and the joy of living out His word. This involves actively seeking out and meditating on the promises found in the Bible, allowing them to infuse our hearts and minds with hope and positivity. By doing so, we can face life's challenges with a joyful spirit, confident that God is with us and His promises are true.

In our daily lives, there are many opportunities to take delight in God's promises and to share that delight with others. It could be through acts of kindness, words of encouragement, or simply sharing a testimony of God's faithfulness in our lives. Each of these actions, when done with a heart full of joy and faith, reflects the sweetness of God's promises to those around us. Just as a well-made Café Bombón brings pleasure and satisfaction, our joyful faith can bring encouragement and hope to others.

Walking courageously with the Lord also means being intentional about remembering and celebrating God's goodness. Just as Café

Bombón is a treat to be savored, the moments of God's faithfulness and the fulfillment of His promises are to be cherished and celebrated. This involves keeping a journal of answered prayers, sharing testimonies with friends and family, and giving thanks to God for His blessings. By actively remembering and celebrating God's goodness, we reinforce our faith and inspire others to trust in Him as well.

Another important aspect of a courageous walk with the Lord is the willingness to trust in His promises even when circumstances seem difficult. Just as the sweetness of condensed milk balances the bitterness of espresso in Café Bombón, God's promises provide balance and hope in the midst of life's challenges. This requires us to hold onto our faith and to believe that God's word is true, even when we cannot see the immediate fulfillment of His promises. By trusting in God's timing and His faithfulness, we can navigate difficult times with a hopeful and positive outlook.

Walking courageously with the Lord also means being a source of joy and encouragement to others. Just as Café Bombón brings a smile to those who drink it, our faith and our joy in God's promises should bring encouragement to those around us. We can share scriptures that have been meaningful to us, offer a listening ear, or simply be a positive presence in someone's life. By being a source of joy and encouragement, we reflect the love and grace of God and help others experience His goodness.

Living a life of courageous faith also means finding joy in the small blessings and daily moments of God's faithfulness. Just as the simple pleasure of drinking Café Bombón can bring joy, the small moments of God's provision and care in our lives are to be appreciated and celebrated. This involves being mindful of God's presence in our daily lives, thanking Him for the little things, and finding contentment in His provision. By cultivating an attitude of gratitude and joy, we can maintain a positive and hopeful outlook, regardless of our circumstances.

Walking courageously with the Lord also means sharing our faith and the joy of God's promises with those who may not yet know Him. Just as Café Bombón is a unique and delightful drink that can be shared with friends and family, the good news of God's love and His promises is meant to be shared with the world. This involves being willing to speak about our faith, to share our personal testimonies, and to invite others to experience the goodness of God. By sharing our faith and the joy of God's promises, we can make a positive impact on the lives of others and help them discover the sweetness of a relationship with God.

In conclusion, walking courageously with the Lord is like savoring a cup of Café Bombón, sweet and delightful, symbolizing the sweetness of God's promises. It involves taking delight in God's promises, trusting in His faithfulness, and sharing that joy with others. By valuing God's promises and making them a central part of our lives, we demonstrate our trust in Him and our desire to live out His word. Remember, as Psalm 34:8 says, "O taste and see that the Lord is good: blessed is the man that trusteth in him." This verse is a powerful reminder to experience the goodness of God and to find our blessings in trusting Him. So, let us take that courageous walk with the Lord, knowing that He is our strength and our guide, and let our lives be a testament to the sweetness and joy of God's promises. Just as a well-made Café Bombón brings delight and satisfaction, our joyful and faithful walk with God can bring encouragement, hope, and inspiration to those around us, making our world a better and brighter place.

Chapter 12 Black Coffee (USA)

"But I fear, lest by any means, as the serpent beguiled Eve through his subtilty, so your minds should be corrupted

from the simplicity that is in Christ." (2 Corinthians 11:3)

Ingredients:

- 2 tablespoons ground coffee
- 1 cup hot water

Equipment:

- Coffee maker or French press

Instructions:

1. Add ground coffee to the coffee maker or French press.
2. Pour hot water over the coffee grounds.
3. If using a coffee maker, follow the machine's instructions. If using a French press, let it steep for 4 minutes, then press the plunger down slowly.
4. Pour the coffee into a cup and serve immediately.

Walking courageously with the Lord can be compared to enjoying a cup of black coffee, simple and straightforward, symbolizing the purity and simplicity found in Christ. Black coffee, unadorned by milk or sugar, provides a clear, unaltered taste, much like how our faith in Christ should be—pure, uncomplicated, and direct. The Bible warns us in 2 Corinthians 11:3, "But I fear, lest by any means, as the serpent beguiled Eve through his subtilty, so your minds should be corrupted from the simplicity that is in Christ." This verse reminds us of the importance of maintaining a straightforward and pure faith, free from unnecessary complications and distractions. Just as black coffee offers a direct and unembellished experience, our relationship with Christ should be marked by clarity and sincerity, focusing on the core truths of the Gospel without being muddled by extraneous matters.

Imagine starting your day with a cup of black coffee. The bold, robust flavor wakes you up and prepares you for the tasks ahead. In the same way, starting our day with prayer and reflection on the simplicity of the Gospel can ground us in our faith and provide us with the strength and clarity needed to navigate the complexities of life. A man who walks courageously with the Lord values the simplicity of Christ's teachings and strives to keep his faith straightforward and focused. This involves adhering to the basic principles of love, grace, and truth as taught by Jesus, and not allowing ourselves to be distracted or led astray by false teachings or complicated doctrines that can cloud our understanding.

Walking courageously with the Lord means embracing the purity and simplicity of our faith. Just as black coffee is free from additives, our faith should be free from anything that detracts from the core message of the Gospel. This requires us to focus on the essentials—loving God, loving others, and living according to God's commandments. By keeping our faith simple and straightforward, we can avoid the pitfalls of overcomplicating our beliefs and stay true to the foundational truths that Jesus taught.

In our daily lives, there are many opportunities to practice and maintain a simple and straightforward faith. It could be through honest and heartfelt prayer, reading the Bible with an open and teachable spirit, or living out our faith through acts of kindness and service. Each of these actions, when done with a heart focused on the simplicity of Christ, helps to strengthen our relationship with God and keep our faith pure. Just as a cup of black coffee provides a clear and unambiguous flavor, our simple and sincere faith can provide clarity and direction in our lives.

Walking courageously with the Lord also means being vigilant against anything that could complicate or corrupt our faith. Just as black coffee can become diluted or altered if other ingredients are added, our faith can become weakened if we allow ourselves to be influenced by false teachings or distracted by worldly concerns. This requires us to be discerning and to hold fast to the truth of the Gospel, rejecting anything that does not align with God's word. By guarding our hearts and minds against such influences, we can maintain a pure and straightforward faith that is pleasing to God.

Another important aspect of a courageous walk with the Lord is the willingness to simplify our lives in order to focus more fully on our relationship with Him. Just as black coffee is a simple and unadorned beverage, our lives should reflect a simplicity that prioritizes our faith and relationship with God above all else. This might involve simplifying our schedules, reducing our commitments, or letting go of material possessions that distract us from our spiritual goals. By simplifying our lives, we create more space for God and allow ourselves to grow deeper in our faith.

Walking courageously with the Lord also means being content with the simplicity of His provision. Just as black coffee is appreciated for its pure and unembellished flavor, we should appreciate the simple and profound blessings that God provides. This involves cultivating an attitude of gratitude and contentment, recognizing that God's provision is sufficient for our needs. By focusing on the simplicity of God's blessings, we can avoid the trap of constantly seeking more and instead find joy and satisfaction in what we have been given.

Living a life of courageous faith also means being straightforward and honest in our dealings with others. Just as black coffee is straightforward in its presentation, our interactions with others should be marked by honesty, integrity, and transparency. This involves speaking the truth in love, being reliable and trustworthy, and living in a way that reflects the simplicity and purity of Christ. By being straightforward and honest, we build trust and credibility with others, making our witness for Christ more effective.

Walking courageously with the Lord also means being open to the simplicity of His guidance and direction. Just as black coffee offers a clear and direct flavor, God's guidance is often simple and straightforward, though not always easy to follow. This requires us to listen attentively to His voice, to be obedient to His commands, and to trust in His leading, even when it seems counterintuitive or challenging. By embracing the simplicity of God's guidance, we can navigate life's complexities with confidence and clarity.

In conclusion, walking courageously with the Lord is like enjoying a cup of black coffee, simple and straightforward, symbolizing the purity and simplicity found in Christ. It involves maintaining a pure and uncomplicated faith, focusing on the core truths of the Gospel, and avoiding anything that might complicate or corrupt our beliefs. By valuing the simplicity of Christ's teachings and living out our faith with clarity and sincerity, we demonstrate our commitment to God and our desire to follow Him faithfully. Remember, as 2 Corinthians 11:3 warns, we must guard against anything that seeks to corrupt the simplicity that is in Christ. So, let us take that courageous walk with the Lord, knowing that He is our strength and our guide, and let our lives be a testament to the purity and simplicity of a faith that is focused on the essentials. Just as a well-brewed cup of black coffee can provide clarity and energy, our straightforward and sincere walk with God can bring clarity, strength, and inspiration to our lives and to those around us, making our world a better and brighter place. By keeping our faith pure and uncomplicated, we honor God and reflect the simplicity and purity of Christ in all that we do.

Chapter 13 Café Touba (Senegal)

"For we are unto God a sweet savour of Christ, in them that are saved, and in them that perish." (2 Corinthians

2:15)

Ingredients:

- 1 cup water
- 1 tablespoon finely ground coffee
- 1/4 teaspoon ground Guinea pepper (djar)
- Sugar (optional, to taste)

Equipment:

- Small saucepan
- Coffee filter or fine mesh sieve

Instructions:

1. In a small saucepan, bring the water to a boil.
2. Add the ground coffee and Guinea pepper to the boiling water.
3. Reduce the heat and simmer for about 5 minutes.
4. Remove from heat and let it steep for another 5 minutes.
5. Strain the coffee through a filter or sieve into a cup.
6. Add sugar to taste, if desired.
7. Serve hot.

Walking courageously with the Lord can be compared to savoring a cup of Café Touba, a traditional Senegalese coffee that is spiced and aromatic, symbolizing the fragrance of a faithful life. Café Touba is unique due to its blend of coffee and Guinea pepper, which creates a rich, spicy aroma and a bold flavor that lingers. This special blend not only awakens the senses but also symbolizes how our lives, when filled with faith, righteousness, and good deeds, can be a pleasing aroma to God and to those around us. The Bible tells us in 2 Corinthians 2:15, "For we are unto God a sweet savour of Christ, in them that are saved, and in them that perish." This verse reminds us that our lives should emit the sweet fragrance of Christ, reflecting His love, grace, and righteousness in all we do. Just as the spices in Café Touba enhance its flavor and aroma, our good deeds and faithful living enhance our witness for Christ, making our lives a testament to His goodness and transformative power.

Imagine starting your day with a cup of Café Touba. The warm, spiced aroma fills your home, and the first sip is a delightful blend of flavors that invigorate your spirit. In the same way, starting our day with prayer and reflection on God's word can fill our hearts with His presence and prepare us for the day ahead. A man who walks courageously with the Lord lives a life that is not only strong in faith but also rich in good deeds and righteousness. This kind of life is like a pleasing aroma that draws others to God, inspiring them to seek Him and experience His love. Walking courageously with the Lord means being intentional about filling our lives with the fragrance of Christ. This involves living out our faith in tangible ways, through acts of kindness, compassion, and integrity. Just as the spices in Café Touba are carefully chosen and blended to create a unique flavor, our actions and attitudes should be chosen to reflect Christ's love and righteousness. Every kind word, every act of service, and every moment of integrity adds to the pleasing aroma of our lives, making us effective witnesses for Christ.

In our daily lives, there are countless opportunities to let the fragrance of our faith shine through. It could be through helping a neighbor, volunteering at a local charity, or simply being a source of encouragement to someone who is struggling. Each of these actions, when done with a heart full of faith, reflects the love and grace of God. Just as a wellmade cup of Café Touba brings comfort and warmth, our lives can bring comfort and hope to those around us when we live out our faith with authenticity and love. Walking courageously with the Lord also means being mindful of how our actions affect others. Just as the aroma of Café Touba can fill a room and uplift those who smell it, our lives should positively impact those around us. This requires us to be intentional about our choices and to strive for excellence in all we do. Whether we are at work, at home, or in our communities, we should aim to reflect the character of Christ in every situation. This kind of intentional living not only honors God but also draws others to Him.

Another important aspect of a courageous walk with the Lord is the willingness to stand out and be different. Just as Café Touba stands out because of its unique blend of spices, our lives should stand out because of our commitment to Christ and our distinctive way of living. This might mean making choices that are counter-cultural or taking a stand for what is right, even when it is not popular. By living according to God's principles and being willing to be different, we set an example for others and demonstrate the transformative power of faith. Walking courageously with the Lord also involves being a source of encouragement and support to others. Just as the spices in Café Touba add warmth and depth to the coffee, our words and actions can add warmth and depth to the lives of those around us. We can offer a listening ear, a word of encouragement, or a helping hand to someone in need. By being a source of support and encouragement, we reflect the love of Christ and help others experience His grace and kindness.

Living a life of courageous faith also means being consistent in our walk with God. Just as the process of making Café Touba requires consistency and attention to detail, our spiritual lives require consistency in prayer, Bible study, and worship. This consistency helps us stay grounded in our faith and ensures that our lives continue to reflect the fragrance of Christ. By making a habit of seeking God and aligning our actions with His will, we grow stronger in our faith and become more effective witnesses for Him. Walking courageously with the Lord also means being grateful for the unique blend of gifts and experiences He has given us. Just as each ingredient in Café Touba contributes to its unique flavor, each of our gifts and experiences contributes to who we are and how we can serve God. Embracing our individuality and using our gifts for God's glory allows us to live fulfilling and impactful lives. By recognizing and appreciating the unique ways God has equipped us, we can make the most of every opportunity to serve Him and others.

In conclusion, walking courageously with the Lord is like enjoying a cup of Café Touba, spiced and aromatic, filled with the rich fragrance of a faithful life. It involves living out our faith in tangible ways, being intentional about our actions, and striving to reflect the character of Christ in all we do. By letting our lives be a pleasing aroma to God, filled with righteousness and good deeds, we can be effective witnesses for Christ and make a positive impact on the world around us. Remember, as 2 Corinthians 2:15 says, "For we are unto God a sweet savour of Christ, in them that are saved, and in them that perish." This verse is a powerful reminder that our lives should emit the sweet fragrance of Christ, drawing others to Him and reflecting His love and grace. So, let us take that courageous walk with the Lord, knowing that He is our strength and our guide, and let our lives be a testament to the rich, varied, and beautiful aroma of a faithful life. Just as a well-made cup of Café Touba can warm the heart and soul, our faithful living can bring warmth, comfort, and joy to those around us, making our world a better and brighter place. Walking courageously with the Lord involves living a life that reflects His love, grace, and righteousness, much like the rich aroma of Café Touba that fills the air and draws people in. By being intentional about our actions and striving to reflect the character of Christ, we can make a positive impact on the world around us and inspire others to seek Him. Let us embrace the unique blend of gifts and experiences God has given us and use them for His glory, making the most of every opportunity to serve Him and others. By doing so, we can live a life that is a pleasing aroma to God and a testament to the richness and depth of a faithful life.

Chapter 14 Kaffeost (Sweden/Finland)

"Come unto me, all ye that labour and are heavy laden, and I will give you rest." Matthew 11:28

Ingredients:

- 1 cup strong brewed coffee
- 1-2 pieces of Finnish cheese (Leipäjuusto or "bread cheese")

Equipment:

- Coffee maker or French press
- Cup or mug

Instructions:

1. Brew a strong cup of coffee.
2. Place pieces of cheese in a cup or mug.
3. Pour the hot coffee over the cheese.
4. Let the cheese soften and enjoy the coffee as it becomes infused with the cheese flavor.
5. Serve immediately.

Walking courageously with the Lord can be compared to savoring a cup of Kaffeost, a unique and comforting beverage from Sweden and Finland that combines hot coffee with pieces of cheese, symbolizing the uniqueness and comfort found in Christ. Kaffeost, also known as "coffee cheese," is a traditional drink where warm, rich coffee is poured over chunks of cheese, typically a type called leipäjuusto or "bread cheese," which softens and absorbs the coffee, creating a soothing and delightful experience. This unique combination reflects how Christ brings comfort and peace into our lives in ways that are often unexpected and deeply personal. The Bible invites us in Matthew 11:28, "Come unto me, all ye that labour and are heavy laden, and I will give you rest." This verse reminds us of the rest and comfort that Christ offers to all who come to Him, much like the comforting and unique experience of enjoying Kaffeost. Just as the warm coffee and cheese create a special blend that soothes and satisfies, Christ's presence in our lives brings a unique comfort and peace that cannot be found anywhere else.

Imagine starting your day with a cup of Kaffeost. The process of making it involves heating the coffee and carefully adding the cheese, allowing the flavors to meld and create a comforting drink. In the same way, starting our day by coming to Christ and seeking His presence can fill our hearts with peace and prepare us for the challenges ahead. A man who walks courageously with the Lord recognizes the unique ways Christ brings comfort and peace into his life and embraces these moments of rest and reassurance. This kind of faith is not only about enduring hardships but also about finding and cherishing the moments of comfort that Christ provides.

Walking courageously with the Lord means embracing the unique and comforting ways Christ works in our lives. Just as Kaffeost is a distinctive drink that combines unexpected ingredients, our relationship with Christ often involves experiencing His love and comfort in surprising and personal ways. This requires us to be open to the ways Christ might choose to comfort and guide us, whether through His word, through prayer, or through the support of other believers. By being attentive to these moments, we can fully experience the peace and rest that Christ offers.

In our daily lives, there are many opportunities to embrace the unique comfort that Christ provides. It could be through quiet moments of prayer, reading a passage of scripture that speaks to our hearts, or spending time in nature and feeling God's presence around us. Each of these experiences, when done with a heart open to Christ, helps to strengthen our relationship with Him and bring His peace into our lives. Just as a cup of Kaffeost brings warmth and comfort, our moments with Christ can bring a sense of calm and reassurance.

Walking courageously with the Lord also means being intentional about seeking His comfort and peace. Just as making Kaffeost requires a deliberate effort to prepare the coffee and cheese, seeking Christ's presence requires us to set aside time to connect with Him. This involves making prayer and Bible study a regular part of our routine, attending church, and participating in fellowship with other believers. By making these practices a priority, we create space in our lives for Christ to bring His unique comfort and peace.

Another important aspect of a courageous walk with the Lord is the willingness to share the comfort and peace we receive from Christ with others. Just as Kaffeost is often shared and enjoyed with friends and family, the comfort we find in Christ is meant to be shared. This could involve offering a listening ear to someone who is struggling, sharing a scripture that has been meaningful to us, or simply being a calming and supportive presence in someone's life. By sharing the comfort and peace of Christ, we reflect His love and grace to those around us.

Walking courageously with the Lord also means finding comfort in His promises and trusting in His faithfulness. Just as the unique combination of coffee and cheese in Kaffeost creates a special experience, the promises of Christ provide a unique source of comfort and hope. This requires us to hold onto the truths of scripture and to trust that Christ will fulfill His promises, even when we face difficult circumstances. By placing our trust in Christ, we can experience His peace and comfort, knowing that He is in control and that He cares for us deeply.

Living a life of courageous faith also means being open to the ways Christ might use our experiences to bring comfort to others. Just as the process of making Kaffeost involves transforming simple ingredients into a comforting drink, Christ can use our experiences, both good and bad, to bring comfort and encouragement to others. This involves being willing to share our stories and to use our experiences to support and uplift those who are going through similar challenges. By doing so, we allow Christ to work through us to bring His comfort and peace to others.

Walking courageously with the Lord also involves being grateful for the unique ways He brings comfort into our lives. Just as each cup of Kaffeost is a unique and special experience, each moment of comfort from Christ is a gift to be cherished. This involves cultivating an attitude of gratitude and taking time to thank Christ for His presence and His care. By being mindful of these moments, we can fully appreciate the depth of Christ's love and the peace that He brings.

In conclusion, walking courageously with the Lord is like enjoying a cup of Kaffeost, unique and comforting, symbolizing the uniqueness and comfort found in Christ. It involves embracing the unique ways Christ brings comfort and peace into our lives, seeking His presence intentionally, and sharing His comfort with others. By valuing the unique comfort that Christ provides and making it a central part of our lives, we demonstrate our trust in Him and our desire to rest in His care. Remember, as Matthew 11:28 invites us, "Come unto me, all ye that labour and are heavy laden, and I will give you rest." This verse is a powerful reminder of the rest and comfort that Christ offers to all who come to Him. So, let us take that courageous walk with the Lord, knowing that He is our strength and our guide, and let our lives be a testament to the unique and comforting presence of Christ. Just as a well-made cup of Kaffeost brings warmth and comfort, our faithful walk with Christ can bring peace, reassurance, and inspiration to those around us, making our world a better and brighter place. By embracing the unique ways Christ brings comfort and peace into our lives, we honor Him and reflect His love and grace in all that we do.

Chapter 15 Mazagran (Portugal)

"But the Comforter, which is the Holy Ghost, whom the

Father will send in my name, he shall teach you all things, and bring all things to your remembrance, whatsoever I have said unto you." John 14:26

Ingredients:

- 1 cup strong brewed coffee, chilled
- 1 tablespoon lemon juice
- Ice cubes
- Sugar (optional, to taste)
- Lemon slices for garnish

Equipment:

- Coffee maker or French press
- Glass

Instructions:

1. Brew a strong cup of coffee and let it chill.
2. In a glass, combine the chilled coffee and lemon juice.
3. Add ice cubes to the glass.
4. Add sugar to taste, if desired.
5. Garnish with lemon slices.
6. Serve cold.

Walking courageously with the Lord can be compared to savoring a glass of Mazagran, a refreshing and invigorating Portuguese coffee drink that blends strong coffee with lemon juice and sometimes soda water, symbolizing the refreshing presence of the Holy Spirit in our lives. Mazagran is known for its unique and revitalizing taste, offering a cool and energizing experience that is both surprising and delightful. Similarly, our walk with the Lord should be marked by the refreshing and invigorating influence of the Holy Spirit, who brings new life, energy, and clarity to our spiritual journey. The Bible tells us in John 14:26, "But the Comforter, which is the Holy Ghost, whom the Father will send in my name, he shall teach you all things, and bring all things to your remembrance, whatsoever I have said unto you." This verse reminds us of the role of the Holy Spirit as our teacher and guide, bringing to mind the truths of God's word and refreshing our spirits with His presence, much like how Mazagran refreshes and revitalizes on a hot day.

Imagine starting your day with a glass of Mazagran. The process of making it involves brewing strong coffee, adding a splash of lemon juice, and sometimes mixing in soda water, creating a drink that is both invigorating and refreshing. In the same way, starting our day by inviting the Holy Spirit to fill us and guide us can invigorate our spiritual lives and prepare us for the challenges ahead. A man who walks courageously with the Lord recognizes the importance of the Holy Spirit's presence and seeks to be continually refreshed and guided by Him. This kind of faith is not only about enduring hardships but also about experiencing the renewal and vitality that comes from the Holy Spirit.

Walking courageously with the Lord means allowing the Holy Spirit to refresh and invigorate our spiritual lives. Just as Mazagran is a blend of coffee and lemon that creates a unique and revitalizing experience, our relationship with the Holy Spirit involves experiencing His guidance, comfort, and empowerment in new and dynamic ways. This requires us to be open to the Holy Spirit's work in our lives, to listen for His voice, and to follow His leading. By being attentive to the Holy Spirit, we can experience a refreshing and invigorating faith that sustains us through all of life's challenges.

In our daily lives, there are many opportunities to allow the Holy Spirit to refresh and invigorate our spiritual lives. It could be through moments of quiet reflection, times of worship, or periods of intense prayer. Each of these experiences, when done with a heart open to the Holy Spirit, helps to renew our spirits and strengthen our faith. Just as a glass of Mazagran provides a refreshing break on a hot day, the presence of the Holy Spirit can bring a sense of peace, clarity, and energy to our lives.

Walking courageously with the Lord also means being intentional about seeking the Holy Spirit's guidance and presence. Just as making Mazagran requires a deliberate effort to prepare the coffee and lemon juice, seeking the Holy Spirit requires us to set aside time to connect with Him. This involves making prayer, worship, and Bible study regular parts of our routine, and being open to the ways the Holy Spirit might speak to us. By making these practices a priority, we create space in our lives for the Holy Spirit to refresh and invigorate us.

Another important aspect of a courageous walk with the Lord is the willingness to be led by the Holy Spirit, even when it means stepping out of our comfort zones. Just as Mazagran is a unique and unexpected blend of flavors, the Holy Spirit often leads us in ways that are surprising and challenging.

This requires us to trust in His guidance and to be willing to follow His leading, even when it is difficult or uncomfortable. By being open to the Holy Spirit's direction, we can experience new levels of growth and vitality in our faith.

Walking courageously with the Lord also means being a source of refreshment and encouragement to others. Just as Mazagran provides a refreshing and invigorating experience, our faith and our relationship with the Holy Spirit should bring encouragement and renewal to those around us. We can offer a listening ear, share a word of encouragement, or simply be a calming and supportive presence in someone's life. By being a source of refreshment and encouragement, we reflect the love and grace of God and help others experience the refreshing presence of the Holy Spirit.

Living a life of courageous faith also means being open to the ways the Holy Spirit wants to work through us to impact others. Just as the process of making Mazagran involves combining different ingredients to create a refreshing drink, the Holy Spirit can use our unique gifts and experiences to bring renewal and encouragement to others. This involves being willing to share our stories, to use our gifts to serve others, and to be a vessel through which the Holy Spirit can work. By being open to the Holy Spirit's work, we can make a positive impact on the lives of others and help them experience the refreshing presence of God.

Walking courageously with the Lord also involves being grateful for the ways the Holy Spirit refreshes and invigorates our lives. Just as each glass of Mazagran is a unique and special experience, each moment of the Holy Spirit's presence is a gift to be cherished. This involves cultivating an attitude of gratitude and taking time to thank the Holy Spirit for His guidance, comfort, and empowerment. By being mindful of these moments, we can fully appreciate the depth of God's love and the peace that the Holy Spirit brings.

In conclusion, walking courageously with the Lord is like enjoying a glass of Mazagran, refreshing and invigorating, symbolizing the refreshing presence of the Holy Spirit. It involves allowing the Holy Spirit to refresh and invigorate our spiritual lives, seeking His presence intentionally, and being open to His guidance. By valuing the refreshing presence of the Holy Spirit and making it a central part of our lives, we demonstrate our trust in God and our desire to be led by Him. Remember, as John 14:26 tells us, the Holy Spirit, our Comforter, teaches us all things and brings to our remembrance everything Jesus has said to us. This verse is a powerful reminder of the vital role the Holy Spirit plays in our lives, much like the refreshing and invigorating experience of Mazagran. So, let us take that courageous walk with the Lord, knowing that He is our strength and our guide, and let our lives be a testament to the refreshing and invigorating presence of the Holy Spirit. Just as a well-made Mazagran brings delight and renewal, our faithful walk with the Holy Spirit can bring encouragement, hope, and inspiration to those around us, making our world a better and brighter place. By embracing the refreshing presence of the Holy Spirit, we honor God and reflect His love and grace in all that we do.

Chapter 16 Café Brasileiro (Brazil)

"For I am not ashamed of the gospel of Christ: for it is the power of God unto salvation to every one that believeth." Romans 1:16

Ingredients:

- 1 cup water
- 1 tablespoon finely ground Brazilian coffee
- Sugar (optional, to taste)

Equipment:

- Small saucepan
- Coffee filter or fine mesh sieve

Instructions:

1. In a small saucepan, bring the water to a boil.
2. Add the ground coffee to the boiling water.
3. Reduce the heat and simmer for about 5 minutes.
4. Remove from heat and let it steep for another 5 minutes.
5. Strain the coffee through a filter or sieve into a cup.
6. Add sugar to taste, if desired.
7. Serve hot.

Walking courageously with the Lord can be compared to savoring a cup of Café Brasileiro, a bold and vibrant Brazilian coffee that is strong and full of flavor, symbolizing the boldness required in sharing the gospel. Café Brasileiro is known for its intense and robust taste, providing a powerful and invigorating experience with each sip. Similarly, our walk with the Lord should be marked by the boldness and confidence we have in sharing the gospel of Christ. The Bible tells us in Romans 1:16, "For I am not ashamed of the gospel of Christ:

for it is the power of God unto salvation to every one that believeth." This verse reminds us of the transformative power of the gospel and the importance of proclaiming it with boldness and without shame, much like the bold flavor of Café Brasileiro, offering a taste of God's love and power that is meant to be shared widely and confidently. Just as Café Brasileiro is enjoyed for its strong and vibrant character, our faith should be vibrant and dynamic, impacting those around us and bringing the message of salvation to everyone we encounter.

Imagine starting your day with a cup of Café Brasileiro. The process of making it involves brewing strong coffee that awakens your senses and energizes your spirit. In the same way, starting our day by reflecting on the boldness and power of the gospel can fill our hearts with courage and prepare us to share our faith with others. A man who walks courageously with the Lord finds strength in the gospel and lets that strength drive him to live boldly for Christ. This kind of faith is not only about maintaining personal devotion but also about actively and confidently sharing the good news with others, trusting in the power of the gospel to change lives.

Walking courageously with the Lord means being bold and vibrant in our faith, much like the intense flavor of Café Brasileiro. Just as this coffee is appreciated for its strong and unapologetic character, our faith should be marked by a boldness that refuses to shy away from opportunities to share the gospel. This involves being unafraid to speak about our faith, to share our personal testimonies, and to engage in conversations about God's love and salvation. By being bold in our faith, we can make a significant impact on those around us, much like how a strong cup of coffee can invigorate and awaken the senses.

In our daily lives, there are numerous opportunities to be bold and vibrant in sharing the gospel. It could be through initiating conversations about faith with friends and family, participating in outreach activities, or using social media to share encouraging scriptures and testimonies. Each of these actions, when done with a heart full of faith and confidence, reflects the boldness of the gospel to those around us. Just as a well-made Café Brasileiro brings a powerful and invigorating experience, our bold proclamation of the gospel can bring hope and transformation to the lives of others.

Walking courageously with the Lord also means embracing the boldness that comes from knowing the power of the gospel. Just as Café Brasileiro is known for its robust flavor, the gospel is powerful and transformative, bringing salvation and new life to those who believe. This requires us to have confidence in the message we share, trusting that God's word will accomplish what He intends. By having this confidence, we can share the gospel boldly, knowing that it has the power to change hearts and lives.

Another important aspect of a courageous walk with the Lord is the willingness to stand firm in our beliefs, even when faced with opposition or ridicule. Just as Café Brasileiro stands out for its strong and distinct flavor, our faith should stand out for its boldness and clarity. This involves being unapologetic about our faith, standing up for what we believe, and not allowing fear or doubt to silence our witness. By standing firm in our beliefs, we demonstrate the strength and conviction of our faith, much like the boldness of Café Brasileiro.

Walking courageously with the Lord also means being a source of encouragement and inspiration to others. Just as Café Brasileiro provides an invigorating experience, our faith should inspire and uplift those around us. We can offer words of encouragement, share uplifting scriptures, and support others in their faith journeys. By being a source of encouragement, we reflect the love and grace of God and help others experience the boldness and confidence that comes from knowing Him.

Living a life of courageous faith also means finding joy and fulfillment in sharing the gospel. Just as the enjoyment of Café Brasileiro brings a sense of satisfaction, sharing the gospel brings a deep sense of joy and purpose. This involves recognizing the privilege and responsibility we have to share the good news and finding joy in the opportunities to do so.

By embracing this joy, we can approach evangelism with enthusiasm and passion, making a positive impact on the lives of others.

Walking courageously with the Lord also involves being open to the guidance of the Holy Spirit as we share the gospel. Just as the process of making Café Brasileiro requires attention and care, sharing the gospel requires us to be attentive to the leading of the Holy Spirit. This means being sensitive to opportunities to share our faith, listening for the Spirit's guidance in our conversations, and being obedient to His promptings. By being open to the Holy Spirit's guidance, we can share the gospel effectively and with confidence.

In conclusion, walking courageously with the Lord is like enjoying a cup of Café Brasileiro, bold and vibrant, symbolizing the boldness required in sharing the gospel. It involves being bold and confident in our faith, trusting in the power of the gospel, and sharing it with others without shame. By valuing the boldness of the gospel and making it a central part of our lives, we demonstrate our commitment to God and our desire to proclaim His message of salvation. Remember, as Romans 1:16 tells us, "For I am not ashamed of the gospel of Christ: for it is the power of God unto salvation to every one that believeth." This verse is a powerful reminder of the transformative power of the gospel and the importance of sharing it boldly. So, let us take that courageous walk with the Lord, knowing that He is our strength and our guide, and let our lives be a testament to the boldness and power of the gospel. Just as a well-made Café Brasileiro brings delight and energy, our bold and confident walk with God can bring hope, encouragement, and transformation to those around us, making our world a better and brighter place. By embracing the boldness of the gospel and sharing it with confidence, we honor God and reflect His love and grace in all that we do.

Chapter 17 Café con Leche (Spain)

"Come unto me, all ye that labour and are heavy laden, and I will give you rest." (Matthew 11:28)

Ingredients:

- 1 cup strong brewed coffee
- 1 cup hot milk
- Sugar (optional, to taste)

Equipment:

- Coffee maker or French press
- Saucepan

Instructions:

1. Brew a strong cup of coffee.
2. Heat the milk in a saucepan until hot but not boiling.
3. Pour the coffee into a cup.
4. Add the hot milk to the coffee.
5. Stir and add sugar to taste, if desired.
6. Serve immediately.

Walking courageously with the Lord can be compared to enjoying a cup of Café con Leche, a comforting Spanish drink that blends strong coffee with warm milk, symbolizing the nurturing and comforting presence of Christ in our lives. Café con Leche is known for its soothing and satisfying taste, providing a moment of warmth and relaxation with each sip. Similarly, our walk with the Lord should be marked by the comfort and nourishment we find in His presence. The Bible invites us in Matthew 11:28, "Come unto me, all ye that labour and are heavy laden, and I will give you rest." This verse reminds us of the rest and comfort that Christ offers to all who come to Him, much like the comforting blend of coffee and milk in Café con Leche, offering us a taste of His love and peace that is meant to be shared widely and experienced deeply. Just as Café con Leche provides a comforting and nurturing experience, Christ's presence offers us profound peace, rest, and nourishment that should permeate our lives and extend to those around us.

Imagine starting your day with a cup of Café con Leche. The process of making it involves brewing strong coffee and warming the milk, then carefully blending them to create a drink that is both invigorating and soothing. In the same way, starting our day by coming to Christ and seeking His presence can fill our hearts with peace and prepare us for the challenges ahead. A man who walks courageously with the Lord finds comfort in Christ's presence and lets that comfort drive him to live in a way that reflects God's love and care. This kind of faith is not only about enduring hardships but also about finding and cherishing the moments of comfort that Christ provides, much like savoring a warm cup of Café con Leche.

Walking courageously with the Lord means embracing the comfort and nourishment that Christ provides. Just as Café con Leche is a blend of coffee and milk that creates a soothing experience, our relationship with Christ involves experiencing His love, peace, and care in a deep and personal way. This requires us to be open to the ways Christ might choose to comfort and guide us, whether through His word, through prayer, or through the support of other believers. By being attentive to these moments, we can fully experience the peace and rest that Christ offers.

In our daily lives, there are many opportunities to find comfort and nourishment in Christ's presence. It could be through quiet moments of prayer, reading a passage of scripture that speaks to our hearts, or spending time in nature and feeling God's presence around us. Each of these experiences, when done with a heart open to Christ, helps to strengthen our relationship with Him and bring His peace into our lives. Just as a cup of Café con Leche brings warmth and comfort, our moments with Christ can bring a sense of calm and reassurance.

Walking courageously with the Lord also means being intentional about seeking His comfort and peace. Just as making Café con Leche requires a deliberate effort to prepare the coffee and milk, seeking Christ's presence requires us to set aside time to connect with Him. This involves making prayer and Bible study a regular part of our routine, attending church, and participating in fellowship with other believers. By making these practices a priority, we create space in our lives for Christ to bring His unique comfort and peace.

Another important aspect of a courageous walk with the Lord is the willingness to share the comfort and peace we receive from Christ with others. Just as Café con Leche is often shared and enjoyed with friends and family, the comfort we find in Christ is meant to be shared. This could involve offering a listening ear to someone who is struggling, sharing a scripture that has been meaningful to us, or simply being a calming and supportive presence in someone's life. By sharing the comfort and peace of Christ, we reflect His love and grace to those around us.

Walking courageously with the Lord also means finding comfort in His promises and trusting in His faithfulness. Just as the blend of coffee and milk in Café con Leche creates a comforting experience, the promises of Christ provide a unique source of comfort and hope. This requires us to hold onto the truths of scripture and to trust that Christ will fulfill His promises, even when we face difficult circumstances. By placing our trust in Christ, we can experience His peace and comfort, knowing that He is in control and that He cares for us deeply.

Living a life of courageous faith also means being open to the ways Christ might use our experiences to bring comfort to others. Just as the process of making Café con Leche involves transforming simple ingredients into a comforting drink, Christ can use our experiences, both good and bad, to bring comfort and encouragement to others. This involves being willing to share our stories and to use our experiences to support and uplift those who are going through similar challenges. By doing so, we allow Christ to work through us to bring His comfort and peace to others.

Walking courageously with the Lord also involves being grateful for the unique ways He brings comfort into our lives. Just as each cup of Café con Leche is a unique and special experience, each moment of comfort from Christ is a gift to be cherished. This involves cultivating an attitude of gratitude and taking time to thank Christ for His presence and His care. By being mindful of these moments, we can fully appreciate the depth of Christ's love and the peace that He brings.

In conclusion, walking courageously with the Lord is like enjoying a cup of Café con Leche, a blend of coffee and milk, symbolizing the nurturing and comforting presence of Christ. It involves finding comfort and nourishment in Christ's presence, seeking His peace intentionally, and sharing His comfort with others. By valuing the unique comfort that

Christ provides and making it a central part of our lives, we demonstrate our trust in Him and our desire to rest in His care. Remember, as Matthew 11:28 invites us, "Come unto me, all ye that labour and are heavy laden, and I will give you rest." This verse is a powerful reminder of the rest and comfort that Christ offers to all who come to Him. So, let us take that courageous walk with the Lord, knowing that He is our strength and our guide, and let our lives be a testament to the unique and comforting presence of Christ. Just as a well-made cup of Café con Leche brings warmth and comfort, our faithful walk with Christ can bring peace, reassurance, and inspiration to those around us, making our world a better and brighter place. By embracing the unique ways Christ brings comfort and peace into our lives, we honor Him and reflect His love and grace in all that we do.

Chapter 18 Affogato (Italy)

"For the law was given by Moses, but grace and truth came by Jesus Christ." John 1:17

Ingredients:

- 1 shot (1.5 oz) hot espresso
- 1 scoop vanilla ice cream

Equipment:

- Espresso machine
- Small bowl or glass

Instructions:

1. Brew a shot of hot espresso.
2. Place a scoop of vanilla ice cream in a small bowl or glass.
3. Pour the hot espresso over the ice cream.
4. Serve immediately and enjoy the combination of hot and cold.

Walking courageously with the Lord can be compared to savoring an affogato, an Italian dessert that blends hot espresso with cold ice cream, symbolizing the balance of grace and truth in Christ. An affogato combines the bold, intense flavor of hot espresso with the creamy sweetness of ice cream, creating a harmonious blend of contrasts that is both refreshing and invigorating. Similarly, our walk with the Lord should be marked by a balance of grace and truth, embodying the fullness of Christ's character. The Bible tells us in John 1:17, "For the law was given by Moses, but grace and truth came by Jesus Christ." This verse reminds us that while the law provides guidance, it is through Jesus that we experience the perfect balance of grace and truth, much like the affogato offers a perfect blend of hot and cold, inviting us to embrace the fullness of His love and wisdom. Just as an affogato provides a unique and delightful experience, living in the balance of grace and truth offers us a life that is rich in love, integrity, and authenticity, and this balance should extend to those around us.

Imagine starting your day with an affogato. The process of making it involves pouring hot espresso over a scoop of cold ice cream, creating a delightful contrast that awakens your senses. In the same way, starting our day by reflecting on the balance of grace and truth in Christ can fill our hearts with His love and wisdom, preparing us to navigate the complexities of life with integrity and compassion. A man who walks courageously with the Lord recognizes the importance of embracing both grace and truth in his life, allowing these qualities to guide his actions and relationships. This kind of faith is not only about adhering to the truth but also about extending grace to others, much like savoring the hot and cold blend of an affogato.

Walking courageously with the Lord means experiencing and sharing the balance of grace and truth. Just as an affogato is a blend of hot espresso and cold ice cream that creates a unique and refreshing experience, our relationship with Christ involves living out His truth while extending His grace.

This requires us to hold firm to the teachings of the Bible while also showing compassion and forgiveness to those around us. By doing so, we can reflect the fullness of Christ's character, much like how an affogato reflects the perfect blend of contrasting elements.

In our daily lives, there are numerous opportunities to experience and share the balance of grace and truth. It could be through standing up for what is right while also being understanding and forgiving of others' mistakes, or through having honest conversations that are also filled with empathy and kindness. Each of these actions, when done with a heart full of faith and love, reflects the balance of grace and truth to those around us. Just as a well-made affogato brings a delightful and harmonious experience, our balanced approach to life can bring peace and harmony to our relationships and interactions.

Walking courageously with the Lord also means being intentional about cultivating both grace and truth in our lives. Just as making an affogato requires a deliberate effort to prepare the espresso and ice cream, living in the balance of grace and truth requires us to intentionally seek God's guidance and strength. This involves making prayer, Bible study, and self-reflection regular parts of our routine, and being open to the ways God wants to grow these qualities in us. By making these practices a priority, we create space in our lives for Christ to shape us into His likeness, balancing grace and truth in all we do.

Another important aspect of a courageous walk with the Lord is the willingness to extend both grace and truth to others. Just as an affogato is often enjoyed and shared with others, the balance of grace and truth we receive from Christ is meant to be shared. This could involve offering forgiveness and understanding in difficult situations, speaking the truth in love, or simply being a source of support and encouragement to those who need it. By sharing the balance of grace and truth, we reflect Christ's love and wisdom to those around us.

Walking courageously with the Lord also means finding strength and guidance in His grace and truth. Just as the blend of hot and cold in an affogato creates a refreshing experience, the balance of grace and truth in Christ provides us with the strength and clarity we need to face life's challenges. This requires us to trust in God's word and rely on His grace to sustain us, even when circumstances are difficult. By placing our trust in Christ, we can navigate life's ups and downs with confidence, knowing that His grace and truth are always with us.

Living a life of courageous faith also means being open to the ways God wants to use us to bring grace and truth to others. Just as the process of making an affogato involves transforming simple ingredients into a delightful treat, God can use our unique gifts and experiences to bring His love and wisdom to others. This involves being willing to share our stories, to use our gifts to serve others, and to be a vessel through which God's grace and truth can flow. By being open to God's work in us and through us, we can make a positive impact on the lives of others and help them experience the balance of grace and truth.

Walking courageously with the Lord also involves being grateful for the ways He balances grace and truth in our lives. Just as each affogato is a unique and special experience, each moment of God's grace and truth is a gift to be cherished. This involves cultivating an attitude of gratitude and taking time to thank God for His presence and His care. By being mindful of these moments, we can fully appreciate the depth of God's love and the wisdom He imparts.

In conclusion, walking courageously with the Lord is like enjoying an affogato, a blend of hot espresso and cold ice cream, symbolizing the balance of grace and truth in Christ. It involves experiencing the balance of grace and truth in our lives, seeking His guidance intentionally, and sharing His love and wisdom with others. By valuing the balance of grace and truth and making it a central part of our lives, we demonstrate our trust in God and our desire to live in His fullness. Remember, as John 1:17 tells us, "For the law was given by Moses, but grace and truth came by Jesus Christ." This verse is a powerful reminder of the completeness we find in Christ, much like the refreshing and harmonious experience of an affogato. So, let us take that courageous walk with the Lord, knowing that He is our strength and our guide, and let our lives be a testament to the balance of grace and truth in Christ. Just as a well-made affogato brings delight and harmony, our balanced walk with God can bring peace, encouragement, and inspiration to those around us, making our world a better and brighter place. By embracing the balance of grace and truth, we honor God and reflect His love and wisdom in all that we do.

Chapter 19 Café Mocha (Morocco)

"For I am persuaded, that neither death, nor life, nor angels, nor principalities, nor powers, nor things present, nor things to come, Nor height, nor depth, nor any other creature,

shall be able to separate us from the love of God, which is in Christ Jesus our Lord." Romans 8:38-39

Ingredients:

- 1 shot (1.5 oz) espresso
- 1 tablespoon cocoa powder
- 1 tablespoon sugar
- 1 cup steamed milk
- Whipped cream (optional)

Equipment:

- Espresso machine
- Milk steamer
- Mug

Instructions:

1. Brew a shot of espresso.
2. In a mug, mix the cocoa powder and sugar.
3. Pour the hot espresso over the cocoa mixture and stir to combine.
4. Add the steamed milk and stir.
5. Top with whipped cream, if desired.
6. Serve immediately.

Walking courageously with the Lord can be compared to savoring a cup of Café Mocha, a delightful Moroccan beverage that blends the boldness of coffee with the richness of chocolate, symbolizing the profound and encompassing love of God. Café Mocha is known for its indulgent and comforting taste, providing a moment of warmth and satisfaction with each sip. Similarly, our walk with the Lord should be marked by the embrace of God's rich and unending love, which is meant to fill our lives with joy, peace, and confidence. The Bible tells us in Romans 8:38-39, "For I am persuaded, that neither death, nor life, nor angels, nor principalities, nor powers, nor things present, nor things to come, Nor height, nor depth, nor any other creature, shall be able to separate us from the love of God, which is in Christ Jesus our Lord." This verse reminds us of the inseparable and all-encompassing nature of God's love, much like the blend of coffee and chocolate in a Café Mocha, offering us a taste of His love that is meant to be savored deeply and shared generously.

Imagine starting your day with a cup of Café Mocha. The process of making it involves brewing strong coffee and mixing it with rich, velvety chocolate, creating a drink that is both invigorating and soothing. In the same way, starting our day by reflecting on the richness of God's love can fill our hearts with His presence and prepare us to face the day with courage and assurance. A man who walks courageously with the Lord finds strength in the knowledge of God's unwavering love and lets that love guide his actions and interactions. This kind of faith is not only about enduring hardships but also about finding joy in the richness of God's love and sharing that joy with others.

Walking courageously with the Lord means embracing the richness of God's love in our lives and sharing it with others. Just as Café Mocha is a blend of flavors that creates a comforting and indulgent experience, our relationship with Christ involves experiencing His love in all its fullness and allowing that love to overflow to those around us. This requires us to be open to the ways God wants to demonstrate His love to us, whether through His word, through prayer, or through the kindness and support of others. By being attentive to these moments, we can fully experience the depth of God's love and share that love with others in meaningful ways.

In our daily lives, there are many opportunities to embrace the richness of God's love and to share that love with others.

It could be through acts of kindness, words of encouragement, or simply being present for someone in need. Each of these actions, when done with a heart full of God's love, reflects the richness of His love to those around us. Just as a well-made Café Mocha brings warmth and comfort, our loving actions can bring a sense of peace and joy to others.

Walking courageously with the Lord also means being intentional about seeking God's love and allowing it to transform us. Just as making Café Mocha requires a deliberate effort to blend the coffee and chocolate, experiencing God's love requires us to set aside time to connect with Him. This involves making prayer and Bible study a regular part of our routine, attending church, and participating in fellowship with other believers. By making these practices a priority, we create space in our lives for God's love to fill us and to overflow to those around us.

Another important aspect of a courageous walk with the Lord is the willingness to share the richness of God's love with others, especially those who may not yet know Him. Just as Café Mocha is often enjoyed and shared with friends and family, the love we receive from God is meant to be shared. This could involve sharing our faith, offering support to someone going through a tough time, or simply being a loving and compassionate presence in someone's life. By sharing the richness of God's love, we reflect His grace and compassion to those around us.

Walking courageously with the Lord also means finding strength and assurance in the knowledge that nothing can separate us from God's love. Just as the blend of coffee and chocolate in Café Mocha creates a comforting experience, the assurance of God's unwavering love provides us with the strength and confidence we need to face life's challenges. This requires us to trust in God's promises and to rely on His love to sustain us, even when circumstances are difficult. By placing our trust in God's love, we can navigate life's ups and downs with courage and peace.

Living a life of courageous faith also means being open to the ways God wants to use us to demonstrate His love to others. Just as the process of making Café Mocha involves transforming simple ingredients into a delightful drink, God can use our unique gifts and experiences to bring His love to others. This involves being willing to share our stories, to use our gifts to serve others, and to be a vessel through which God's love can flow. By being open to God's work in us and through us, we can make a positive impact on the lives of others and help them experience the richness of God's love.

Walking courageously with the Lord also involves being grateful for the ways He shows His love to us. Just as each cup of Café Mocha is a unique and special experience, each moment of God's love is a gift to be cherished. This involves cultivating an attitude of gratitude and taking time to thank God for His presence and His care. By being mindful of these moments, we can fully appreciate the depth of God's love and the peace that comes from knowing we are loved by Him.

In conclusion, walking courageously with the Lord is like enjoying a cup of Café Mocha, a blend of coffee and chocolate, symbolizing the richness of God's love. It involves embracing the richness of God's love in our lives, seeking His presence intentionally, and sharing His love with others. By valuing the richness of God's love and making it a central part of our lives, we demonstrate our trust in Him and our desire to live in His fullness. Remember, as Romans 8:38-39 tells us, "For I am persuaded, that neither death, nor life, nor angels, nor principalities, nor powers, nor things present, nor things to come, Nor height, nor depth, nor any other creature, shall be able to separate us from the love of God, which is in Christ Jesus our Lord." This verse is a powerful reminder of the inseparable and all-encompassing nature of God's love, much like the comforting and indulgent experience of a Café Mocha. So, let us take that courageous walk with the Lord, knowing that He is our strength and our guide, and let our lives be a testament to the richness and depth of God's love. Just as a well-made Café Mocha brings warmth and comfort, our faithful walk with God can bring peace, joy, and inspiration to those around us, making our world a better and brighter place. By embracing the richness of God's love and sharing it with confidence, we honor God and reflect His love and grace in all that we do.

Chapter 20 Café Breva (USA)

"And thine ears shall hear a word behind thee, saying, This is the way, walk ye in it, when ye turn to the right hand, and when ye turn to the left." (Isaiah 30:21)

Ingredients:

- 1 shot (1.5 oz) espresso
- 1/2 cup half-and-half, steamed

Equipment:

- Espresso machine
- Milk steamer
- Mug

Instructions:

1. Brew a shot of espresso.
2. Steam the half-and-half until it is hot and frothy.
3. Pour the espresso into a mug.
4. Add the steamed half-and-half and stir.
5. Serve immediately.

Walking courageously with the Lord can be compared to savoring a cup of Café Breva, a creamy and smooth coffee beverage popular in the USA, symbolizing the smooth path of righteousness that God provides. Café Breva is made with half-and-half cream instead of milk, creating a rich, velvety texture that is both satisfying and comforting. Similarly, our walk with the Lord should be characterized by the smoothness and clarity of the path of righteousness that He lays out for us. The Bible tells us in Isaiah 30:21, "And thine ears shall hear a word behind thee, saying, This is the way, walk ye in it, when ye turn to the right hand, and when ye turn to the left." This verse reminds us of the guidance that God provides, directing our steps and showing us the way to walk in righteousness, much like the creamy and smooth experience of drinking Café Breva, which offers a taste of the clear and comforting direction that God provides in our lives.

Imagine starting your day with a cup of Café Breva. The process of making it involves carefully steaming half-and-half and blending it with strong coffee to create a drink that is both rich and smooth. In the same way, starting our day by seeking God's guidance and reflecting on His righteousness can fill our hearts with peace and clarity, preparing us to navigate the day with confidence and assurance. A man who walks courageously with the Lord finds peace in the knowledge that God is guiding his steps and providing a smooth path for him to follow. This kind of faith is not only about avoiding pitfalls but also about walking confidently in the direction that God has set, much like enjoying the smooth, creamy texture of Café Breva.

Walking courageously with the Lord means embracing the smooth path of righteousness that He provides. Just as Café Breva is a blend of strong coffee and creamy half-and-half that creates a smooth and satisfying experience, our relationship with Christ involves following His guidance and walking in the path of righteousness that He has set before us. This requires us to be attentive to God's voice, to listen for His direction, and to follow His leading, even when the way ahead is not entirely clear. By doing so, we can experience the peace and clarity that comes from walking in God's will, much like the satisfying experience of drinking a well-made Café Breva.

In our daily lives, there are many opportunities to walk in the path of righteousness and to seek God's guidance. It could be through moments of prayer, studying the Bible, or seeking counsel from wise and trusted mentors. Each of these actions, when done with a heart open to God's leading, helps to strengthen our relationship with Him and to ensure that we are walking in the direction that He has set for us. Just as a cup of Café Breva brings comfort and satisfaction, walking in God's path brings a sense of peace and fulfillment.

Walking courageously with the Lord also means being intentional about following His guidance and walking in His ways. Just as making Café Breva requires careful preparation and attention to detail, walking in the path of righteousness requires us to be deliberate and mindful in our actions. This involves making prayer and Bible study a regular part of our routine, attending church, and participating in fellowship with other believers. By making these practices a priority, we create space in our lives for God to guide us and to show us the way to walk in righteousness.

Another important aspect of a courageous walk with the Lord is the willingness to trust in His direction, even when it is challenging or difficult to understand. Just as the smooth and creamy texture of Café Breva is achieved through a careful blending process, the smooth path of righteousness is often achieved through trusting God's process and His timing. This requires us to have faith that God knows what is best for us and to trust that He is leading us in the right direction. By placing our trust in God, we can navigate the challenges of life with confidence and peace, knowing that He is guiding our steps.

Walking courageously with the Lord also means being a source of guidance and encouragement to others. Just as Café Breva provides a comforting and satisfying experience, our faith and our relationship with God should provide encouragement and support to those around us. We can offer words of wisdom, share uplifting scriptures, and be a positive influence in the lives of others. By being a source of guidance and encouragement, we reflect the love and grace of God and help others experience the smooth path of righteousness.

Living a life of courageous faith also means being open to the ways God wants to use us to guide and support others. Just as the process of making Café Breva involves transforming simple ingredients into a delightful drink, God can use our unique gifts and experiences to bring

His guidance and support to others. This involves being willing to share our stories, to use our gifts to serve others, and to be a vessel through which God's love and wisdom can flow. By being open to God's work in us and through us, we can make a positive impact on the lives of others and help them experience the smooth path of righteousness.

Walking courageously with the Lord also involves being grateful for the guidance and direction He provides. Just as each cup of Café Breva is a unique and special experience, each moment of God's guidance is a gift to be cherished. This involves cultivating an attitude of gratitude and taking time to thank God for His presence and His care. By being mindful of these moments, we can fully appreciate the depth of God's love and the peace that comes from knowing we are walking in His will.

In conclusion, walking courageously with the Lord is like enjoying a cup of Café Breva, creamy and smooth, symbolizing the smooth path of righteousness that God provides. It involves walking in the path of righteousness, seeking His guidance intentionally, and sharing His love and wisdom with others. By valuing the smooth path of righteousness and making it a central part of our lives, we demonstrate our trust in God and our desire to live in His will. Remember, as Isaiah 30:21 tells us, "And thine ears shall hear a word behind thee, saying, This is the way, walk ye in it, when ye turn to the right hand, and when ye turn to the left." This verse is a powerful reminder of the guidance that God provides, much like the comforting and satisfying experience of drinking a Café Breva. So, let us take that courageous walk with the Lord, knowing that He is our strength and our guide, and let our lives be a testament to the smooth path of righteousness that He provides. Just as a wellmade Café Breva brings comfort and satisfaction, our faithful walk with God can bring peace, joy, and inspiration to those around us, making our world a better and brighter place. By embracing the smooth path of righteousness and sharing it with confidence, we honor God and reflect His love and grace in all that we do.

Chapter 21 Cafezinho (Brazil)

"Humble yourselves therefore under the mighty hand of God, that he may exalt you in due time." (1 Peter 5:6)

Ingredients:

- 1 cup water
- 2 tablespoons finely ground coffee
- 2 tablespoons sugar

Equipment:

- Small saucepan
- Coffee filter or fine mesh sieve
- Small cups

Instructions:

1. In a small saucepan, bring the water to a boil.
2. Add the sugar and stir until dissolved.
3. Add the ground coffee and stir.
4. Remove from heat and let it steep for a few minutes.
5. Strain the coffee through a filter or sieve into small cups.
6. Serve hot.

Walking courageously with the Lord can be compared to savoring a cup of Cafezinho, a small and strong Brazilian coffee that symbolizes the strength found in humility. Cafezinho is known for its intense flavor despite its small size, offering a powerful and invigorating experience with each sip. Similarly, our walk with the Lord should be marked by a humble spirit that relies on God's strength. The Bible tells us in 1 Peter 5:6, "Humble yourselves therefore under the mighty hand of God, that he may exalt you in due time." This verse reminds us that true strength comes from humbling ourselves before God and trusting in His timing and power, much like the concentrated strength of Cafezinho, offering a taste of the powerful humility that we are called to embody in our lives.

Imagine starting your day with a cup of Cafezinho. The process of making it involves brewing strong coffee in a small amount, creating a drink that is both potent and satisfying. In the same way, starting our day by humbling ourselves before God and seeking His strength can fill our hearts with the courage and determination needed to face the challenges ahead. A man who walks courageously with the Lord finds strength in his humility and lets that strength drive him to live in a way that reflects God's power and grace. This kind of faith is not only about enduring hardships but also about recognizing our dependence on God and finding strength in His presence, much like savoring the small yet powerful taste of Cafezinho.

Walking courageously with the Lord means embracing the strength that comes from humility. Just as Cafezinho is a small yet potent drink that provides a powerful experience, our relationship with Christ involves acknowledging our limitations and relying on His strength to guide us. This requires us to humble ourselves, to recognize our need for God's help, and to trust that His power is made perfect in our weakness. By doing so, we can experience the strength and courage that comes from relying on God, much like the invigorating experience of drinking a well-made Cafezinho.

In our daily lives, there are many opportunities to practice humility and to rely on God's strength. It could be through moments of prayer, confessing our need for God's guidance, or seeking help and support from others. Each of these actions, when done with a heart full of humility and faith, reflects the strength that comes from relying on God. Just as a cup of Cafezinho brings a powerful and satisfying experience, walking in humility and relying on God's strength brings a sense of peace and assurance.

Walking courageously with the Lord also means being intentional about cultivating humility in our lives. Just as making Cafezinho requires careful preparation and attention to detail, living in humility requires us to be deliberate and mindful in our actions. This involves making prayer and Bible study a regular part of our routine, attending church, and participating in fellowship with other believers. By making these practices a priority, we create space in our lives for God to work in us and to strengthen us.

Another important aspect of a courageous walk with the Lord is the willingness to trust in His timing and to wait for His exaltation. Just as the strength of Cafezinho is achieved through a concentrated brewing process, the strength that comes from humility is often developed through patiently waiting on God. This requires us to have faith that God knows what is best for us and to trust that He will lift us up in His perfect timing. By placing our trust in God, we can navigate the challenges of life with confidence and peace, knowing that He is in control.

Walking courageously with the Lord also means being a source of strength and encouragement to others. Just as Cafezinho provides a strong and invigorating experience, our faith and our relationship with God should provide encouragement and support to those around us. We can offer words of wisdom, share uplifting scriptures, and be a positive influence in the lives of others. By being a source of strength and encouragement, we reflect the love and grace of God and help others experience the power of humility.

Living a life of courageous faith also means being open to the ways God wants to use us to strengthen and support others. Just as the process of making Cafezinho involves transforming simple ingredients into a powerful drink, God can use our unique gifts and experiences to bring His strength and support to others. This involves being willing to share our stories, to use our gifts to serve others, and to be a vessel through which God's love and wisdom can flow. By being open to

God's work in us and through us, we can make a positive impact on the lives of others and help them experience the strength that comes from humility.

Walking courageously with the Lord also involves being grateful for the ways He strengthens us. Just as each cup of Cafezinho is a unique and special experience, each moment of God's strength is a gift to be cherished. This involves cultivating an attitude of gratitude and taking time to thank God for His presence and His care. By being mindful of these moments, we can fully appreciate the depth of God's love and the peace that comes from knowing we are walking in His will.

In conclusion, walking courageously with the Lord is like enjoying a cup of Cafezinho, small and strong, symbolizing the strength found in humility. It involves being humble and strong in our faith, relying on God's strength, and trusting in His timing. By valuing the strength that comes from humility and making it a central part of our lives, we demonstrate our trust in God and our desire to live in His will. Remember, as 1 Peter 5:6 tells us, "Humble yourselves therefore under the mighty hand of God, that he may exalt you in due time." This verse is a powerful reminder of the strength that comes from humility, much like the concentrated and invigorating experience of drinking Cafezinho. So, let us take that courageous walk with the Lord, knowing that He is our strength and our guide, and let our lives be a testament to the power of humility. Just as a well-made Cafezinho brings a strong and satisfying experience, our humble walk with God can bring peace, joy, and inspiration to those around us, making our world a better and brighter place. By embracing the strength found in humility and relying on God's strength, we honor Him and reflect His love and grace in all that we do.

Chapter 22 Café Bombón (Spain)

"O taste and see that the Lord is good: blessed is the man that trusteth in him." Psalm 34:8

Ingredients:

- 1 shot (1.5 oz) espresso
- 1.5 oz sweetened condensed milk

Equipment:

- Espresso machine
- Glass or transparent mug

Instructions:

1. Brew a shot of espresso and set aside.
2. Pour the sweetened condensed milk into the bottom of the glass.
3. Slowly pour the espresso over the condensed milk to create two distinct layers.
4. Serve without stirring to maintain the layers.

Walking courageously with the Lord can be compared to savoring a cup of Café Bombón, a delightful Spanish coffee drink that combines the rich bitterness of espresso with the sweet creaminess of condensed milk, symbolizing the sweetness of God's promises. Café Bombón is known for its beautiful layers and its dessert-like taste, providing a moment of joy and indulgence in each sip. Similarly, our walk with the Lord should be marked by the delight we take in His promises and the joy we find in His presence. The Bible tells us in Psalm 34:8, "O taste and see that the Lord is good: blessed is the man that trusteth in him." This verse invites us to experience the goodness of God, much like savoring the sweet and rich flavors of Café Bombón, and to find our blessings in trusting Him. Just as Café Bombón is a treat that brings a smile to our faces, God's promises are sweet and delightful, offering us hope, joy, and encouragement in our journey of faith.

Imagine starting your day with a cup of Café Bombón. The process of making it involves carefully layering espresso and sweetened condensed milk, resulting in a drink that is visually appealing and wonderfully delicious. In the same way, starting our day by reflecting on God's promises can fill our hearts with joy and set a positive tone for the day ahead. A man who walks courageously with the Lord finds joy in God's promises and lets that joy radiate to others. This kind of faith is not only about enduring hardships but also about celebrating the goodness and faithfulness of God.

Walking courageously with the Lord means taking delight in His promises and sharing that delight with others. Just as Café Bombón is a blend of flavors that creates a delightful experience, our faith should be a blend of trust in God's promises and the joy of living out His word. This involves actively seeking out and meditating on the promises found in the Bible, allowing them to infuse our hearts and minds with hope and positivity. By doing so, we can face life's challenges with a joyful spirit, confident that God is with us and His promises are true.

In our daily lives, there are many opportunities to take delight in God's promises and to share that delight with others. It could be through acts of kindness, words of encouragement, or simply sharing a testimony of God's faithfulness in our lives. Each of these actions, when done with a heart full of joy and faith, reflects the sweetness of God's promises to those around us. Just as a well-made Café Bombón brings pleasure and satisfaction, our joyful faith can bring encouragement and hope to others.

Walking courageously with the Lord also means being intentional about remembering and celebrating God's goodness. Just as Café

Bombón is a treat to be savored, the moments of God's faithfulness and the fulfillment of His promises are to be cherished and celebrated. This involves keeping a journal of answered prayers, sharing testimonies with friends and family, and giving thanks to God for His blessings. By actively remembering and celebrating God's goodness, we reinforce our faith and inspire others to trust in Him as well.

Another important aspect of a courageous walk with the Lord is the willingness to trust in His promises even when circumstances seem difficult. Just as the sweetness of condensed milk balances the bitterness of espresso in Café Bombón, God's promises provide balance and hope in the midst of life's challenges. This requires us to hold onto our faith and to believe that God's word is true, even when we cannot see the immediate fulfillment of His promises. By trusting in God's timing and His faithfulness, we can navigate difficult times with a hopeful and positive outlook.

Walking courageously with the Lord also means being a source of joy and encouragement to others. Just as Café Bombón brings a smile to those who drink it, our faith and our joy in God's promises should bring encouragement to those around us. We can share scriptures that have been meaningful to us, offer a listening ear, or simply be a positive presence in someone's life. By being a source of joy and encouragement, we reflect the love and grace of God and help others experience His goodness.

Living a life of courageous faith also means finding joy in the small blessings and daily moments of God's faithfulness. Just as the simple pleasure of drinking Café Bombón can bring joy, the small moments of God's provision and care in our lives are to be appreciated and celebrated. This involves being mindful of God's presence in our daily lives, thanking Him for the little things, and finding contentment in His provision. By cultivating an attitude of gratitude and joy, we can maintain a positive and hopeful outlook, regardless of our circumstances.

Walking courageously with the Lord also means sharing our faith and the joy of God's promises with those who may not yet know Him. Just as Café Bombón is a unique and delightful drink that can be shared with friends and family, the good news of God's love and His promises is meant to be shared with the world. This involves being willing to speak about our faith, to share our personal testimonies, and to invite others to experience the goodness of God. By sharing our faith and the joy of God's promises, we can make a positive impact on the lives of others and help them discover the sweetness of a relationship with God.

In conclusion, walking courageously with the Lord is like savoring a cup of Café Bombón, sweet and delightful, symbolizing the sweetness of God's promises. It involves taking delight in God's promises, trusting in His faithfulness, and sharing that joy with others. By valuing God's promises and making them a central part of our lives, we demonstrate our trust in Him and our desire to live out His word.

Remember, as Psalm 34:8 says, "O taste and see that the Lord is good: blessed is the man that trusteth in him." This verse is a powerful reminder to experience the goodness of God and to find our blessings in trusting Him. So, let us take that courageous walk with the Lord, knowing that He is our strength and our guide, and let our lives be a testament to the sweetness and joy of God's promises. Just as a well-made Café Bombón brings delight and satisfaction, our joyful and faithful walk with God can bring encouragement, hope, and inspiration to those around us, making our world a better and brighter place. By embracing the sweetness of God's promises and sharing it with confidence, we honor God and reflect His love and grace in all that we do.

Chapter 23 Café Zorro (Spain)

"And he said unto me, My grace is sufficient for thee: for my strength is made perfect in weakness." 2 Corinthians 12:9

Ingredients:

- 2 shots (3 oz) espresso
- 3 oz hot water

Equipment:

- Espresso machine
- Cup

Instructions:

1. Brew two shots of espresso.
2. Add hot water to the espresso, maintaining a 1:1 ratio.
3. Serve immediately.

Walking courageously with the Lord can be compared to savoring a cup of Café Zorro, a Spanish coffee known for its double strength, symbolizing the power of faith. Café Zorro is made by combining a double shot of espresso with hot water, creating a strong and bold drink that provides a powerful and invigorating experience. Similarly, our walk with the Lord should be marked by a strong and unwavering faith that relies on God's power. The Bible tells us in 2 Corinthians 12:9, "And he said unto me, My grace is sufficient for thee: for my strength is made perfect in weakness." This verse reminds us that God's grace is enough for us and that His strength is most evident in our weaknesses, much like the concentrated strength of Café Zorro offers a taste of the powerful faith we are called to embody in our lives.

Imagine starting your day with a cup of Café Zorro. The process of making it involves brewing a double shot of espresso and adding hot water, resulting in a drink that is both intense and satisfying. In the same way, starting our day by seeking God's strength and reflecting on His power can fill our hearts with courage and determination needed to face the challenges ahead. A man who walks courageously with the Lord finds strength in his faith and lets that strength drive him to live in a way that reflects God's power and grace. This kind of faith is not only about enduring hardships but also about recognizing our dependence on God and finding strength in His presence, much like savoring the strong and invigorating taste of Café Zorro.

Walking courageously with the Lord means embracing the power that comes from faith. Just as Café Zorro is a strong and bold drink that provides a powerful experience, our relationship with Christ involves acknowledging our limitations and relying on His strength to guide us. This requires us to humble ourselves, to recognize our need for God's help, and to trust that His power is made perfect in our weakness. By doing so, we can experience the strength and courage that comes from relying on God, much like the invigorating experience of drinking a well-made Café Zorro.

In our daily lives, there are many opportunities to practice strengthening our faith and relying on God's power. It could be through moments of prayer, confessing our need for God's guidance, or seeking help and support from others. Each of these actions, when done with a heart full of humility and faith, reflects the strength that comes from relying on God. Just as a cup of Café Zorro brings a powerful and satisfying experience, walking in faith and relying on God's strength brings a sense of peace and assurance.

Walking courageously with the Lord also means being intentional about cultivating a strong faith in our lives. Just as making Café Zorro requires careful preparation and attention to detail, living in faith requires us to be deliberate and mindful in our actions. This involves making prayer and Bible study a regular part of our routine, attending church, and participating in fellowship with other believers. By making these practices a priority, we create space in our lives for God to work in us and to strengthen us.

Another important aspect of a courageous walk with the Lord is the willingness to trust in His power, even when it is challenging or difficult to understand. Just as the strength of Café Zorro is achieved through a concentrated brewing process, the strength that comes from faith is often developed through trusting God's process and His timing. This requires us to have faith that God knows what is best for us and to trust that He is leading us in the right direction. By placing our trust in God, we can navigate the challenges of life with confidence and peace, knowing that He is guiding our steps.

Walking courageously with the Lord also means being a source of strength and encouragement to others. Just as Café Zorro provides a strong and invigorating experience, our faith and our relationship with God should provide encouragement and support to those around us. We can offer words of wisdom, share uplifting scriptures, and be a positive influence in the lives of others. By being a source of strength and encouragement, we reflect the love and grace of God and help others experience the power of faith.

Living a life of courageous faith also means being open to the ways God wants to use us to strengthen and support others. Just as the process of making Café Zorro involves transforming simple ingredients into a powerful drink, God can use our unique gifts and experiences to bring His strength and support to others. This involves being willing to share our stories, to use our gifts to serve others, and to be a vessel through which God's love and wisdom can flow. By being open to God's work in us and through us, we can make a positive impact on the lives of others and help them experience the strength that comes from faith.

Walking courageously with the Lord also involves being grateful for the ways He strengthens us. Just as each cup of Café Zorro is a unique and special experience, each moment of God's strength is a gift to be cherished. This involves cultivating an attitude of gratitude and taking time to thank God for His presence and His care. By being mindful of these moments, we can fully appreciate the depth of God's love and the peace that comes from knowing we are walking in His will.

In conclusion, walking courageously with the Lord is like enjoying a cup of Café Zorro, double strength, symbolizing the power of faith. It involves strengthening our faith, relying on God's power, and trusting in His timing. By valuing the strength that comes from faith and making it a central part of our lives, we demonstrate our trust in God and our desire to live in His will. Remember, as 2 Corinthians 12:9 tells us, "And he said unto me, My grace is sufficient for thee: for my strength is made perfect in weakness." This verse is a powerful reminder of the strength that comes from faith, much like the concentrated and invigorating experience of drinking Café Zorro. So, let us take that courageous walk with the Lord, knowing that He is our strength and our guide, and let our lives be a testament to the power of faith. Just as a well-made Café Zorro brings a strong and satisfying experience, our faithful walk with God can bring peace, joy, and inspiration to those around us, making our world a better and brighter place. By embracing the power of faith and relying on God's strength, we honor Him and reflect His love and grace in all that we do.

Chapter 24 Café Ristretto (Italy)

"Pray without ceasing." 1 Thessalonians 5:17

Ingredients:

- 18-20 grams of finely ground coffee beans
- Fresh, filtered water

Equipment:

- Espresso machine

Instructions:

1. Preheat the espresso machine.
2. Fill the portafilter with finely ground coffee, and tamp it down firmly and evenly.
3. Insert the portafilter into the machine and lock it in place.
4. Start the machine, and let the espresso brew for about 1520 seconds, aiming for a shorter, more concentrated shot.
5. Serve immediately in a pre-warmed espresso cup.

Walking courageously with the Lord can be compared to savoring a cup of Café Ristretto, a short and strong Italian coffee that symbolizes the power of brief but fervent prayer. Café Ristretto is made by using a smaller amount of water with the same amount of coffee grounds as an espresso, resulting in a concentrated and intense flavor. Similarly, our walk with the Lord should be marked by the practice of short, fervent prayers throughout our day, seeking God's strength and guidance in every moment. The Bible tells us in 1 Thessalonians 5:17, "Pray without ceasing." This verse reminds us of the importance of maintaining a constant line of communication with God, much like the concentrated strength of Café Ristretto, offering a taste of the powerful and continuous connection we are called to maintain with our Creator.

Imagine starting your day with a cup of Café Ristretto. The process of making it involves brewing a small amount of water through finely ground coffee, creating a drink that is both strong and satisfying. In the same way, starting our day with a short, fervent prayer can fill our hearts with God's presence and prepare us to face the challenges ahead. A man who walks courageously with the Lord finds strength in his brief but heartfelt prayers and lets that connection with God guide his actions and interactions. This kind of faith is not only about dedicating long periods to prayer but also about recognizing the power of short, sincere prayers throughout the day, much like savoring the intense and invigorating taste of Café Ristretto.

Walking courageously with the Lord means embracing the power of brief but fervent prayer. Just as Café Ristretto is a short and strong drink that provides a powerful experience, our relationship with Christ involves maintaining a continuous connection with Him through short, heartfelt prayers. This requires us to make a habit of turning to God throughout our day, whether in moments of gratitude, need, or reflection. By doing so, we can experience the strength and guidance that comes from a constant line of communication with God, much like the invigorating experience of drinking a well-made Café Ristretto.

In our daily lives, there are many opportunities to practice short, fervent prayers and to seek God's strength. It could be through a quick prayer of thanks before a meal, asking for guidance before a meeting, or seeking comfort in a moment of stress. Each of these prayers, when offered with a sincere heart, reflects our dependence on God and our desire to maintain a close relationship with Him. Just as a cup of Café Ristretto brings a powerful and satisfying experience, practicing short, fervent prayers brings a sense of peace and assurance.

Walking courageously with the Lord also means being intentional about incorporating short, fervent prayers into our daily routine. Just as making Café Ristretto requires careful preparation and attention to detail, maintaining a habit of brief, heartfelt prayers requires us to be deliberate and mindful in our actions. This involves making prayer a natural part of our day, whether we are at home, at work, or in our community. By making these prayers a priority, we create space in our lives for God to work in us and to strengthen us.

Another important aspect of a courageous walk with the Lord is the willingness to trust in the power of brief but fervent prayer, even when it seems insufficient. Just as the strength of Café Ristretto is achieved through a concentrated brewing process, the power of our prayers is often seen in their sincerity and frequency, rather than their length. This requires us to have faith that God hears and responds to our prayers, no matter how brief. By placing our trust in the power of prayer, we can navigate the challenges of life with confidence and peace, knowing that God is with us.

Walking courageously with the Lord also means being a source of encouragement and support to others through prayer. Just as Café Ristretto provides a strong and invigorating experience, our prayers and our relationship with God should provide encouragement and support to those around us. We can offer to pray for others, share uplifting scriptures, and be a positive influence in the lives of others. By being a source of encouragement through prayer, we reflect the love and grace of God and help others experience the power of a continuous connection with Him.

Living a life of courageous faith also means being open to the ways God wants to use our prayers to strengthen and support others. Just as the process of making Café Ristretto involves transforming simple ingredients into a powerful drink, God can use our brief but fervent prayers to bring His strength and support to others. This involves being willing to pray for others, to use our prayers to serve and uplift others, and to be a vessel through which God's love and wisdom can flow.

By being open to God's work in us and through us, we can make a positive impact on the lives of others and help them experience the power of prayer.

Walking courageously with the Lord also involves being grateful for the ways He responds to our prayers. Just as each cup of Café Ristretto is a unique and special experience, each answered prayer is a gift to be cherished. This involves cultivating an attitude of gratitude and taking time to thank God for His presence and His care. By being mindful of these moments, we can fully appreciate the depth of God's love and the peace that comes from knowing we are walking in His will.

In conclusion, walking courageously with the Lord is like enjoying a cup of Café Ristretto, short and strong, symbolizing the power of brief but fervent prayer. It involves practicing short, fervent prayers throughout our day, seeking God's strength, and trusting in His power. By valuing the strength that comes from brief but heartfelt prayers and making them a central part of our lives, we demonstrate our trust in God and our desire to maintain a continuous connection with Him. Remember, as 1 Thessalonians 5:17 tells us, "Pray without ceasing." This verse is a powerful reminder of the importance of maintaining a constant line of communication with God, much like the concentrated and invigorating experience of drinking Café Ristretto. So, let us take that courageous walk with the Lord, knowing that He is our strength and our guide, and let our lives be a testament to the power of brief but fervent prayer. Just as a well-made Café Ristretto brings a strong and satisfying experience, our faithful walk with God can bring peace, joy, and inspiration to those around us, making our world a better and brighter place. By embracing the power of brief but fervent prayer and relying on God's strength, we honor Him and reflect His love and grace in all that we do.

Chapter 25 Espresso Romano (Italy)

"And of his fulness have all we received, and grace for grace."
John 1:16

Ingredients:

- 1 shot (1.5 oz) espresso
- Lemon twist or slice

Equipment:

- Espresso machine
- Cup

Instructions:

1. Brew a shot of espresso.
2. Add a twist or slice of lemon to the espresso.
3. Serve immediately.

Walking courageously with the Lord can be compared to savoring a cup of Espresso Romano, a strong Italian coffee with a hint of citrus, symbolizing strength with a touch of grace. Espresso Romano combines the bold intensity of espresso with a slice of lemon or a hint of lemon zest, adding a unique twist to the traditional coffee experience. Similarly, our walk with the Lord should be marked by a strong and unwavering faith that is always accompanied by grace. The Bible tells us in John 1:16, "And of his fulness have all we received, and grace for grace." This verse reminds us that we have received the fullness of Christ, including the strength of His presence and the grace that He bestows upon us, much like the bold flavor of espresso complemented by the refreshing touch of citrus in Espresso Romano.

Imagine starting your day with a cup of Espresso Romano. The process of making it involves brewing a strong shot of espresso and adding a touch of lemon, resulting in a drink that is both invigorating and refreshing. In the same way, starting our day by seeking God's strength and reflecting on

His grace can fill our hearts with the courage and compassion needed to face the challenges ahead. A man who walks courageously with the Lord finds strength in his faith and lets that strength be tempered with grace. This kind of faith is not only about standing firm in the face of adversity but also about extending kindness and understanding to others, much like savoring the strong yet refreshing taste of Espresso Romano.

Walking courageously with the Lord means embracing the strength that comes from faith while also carrying a touch of grace with us. Just as Espresso Romano is a blend of strong espresso and the gentle hint of lemon, our relationship with Christ involves being strong in our convictions and actions, while also being gracious and compassionate. This requires us to be firm in our beliefs, to stand up for what is right, and to persevere through trials, while also showing love, forgiveness, and understanding to those around us. By doing so, we can experience the fullness of Christ, much like the invigorating experience of drinking a well-made Espresso Romano.

In our daily lives, there are many opportunities to practice being strong in our faith and carrying a touch of grace. It could be through standing up for someone who is being treated unfairly, offering forgiveness to someone who has wronged us, or showing kindness to a stranger. Each of these actions, when done with a heart full of faith and grace, reflects the strength and compassion of Christ. Just as a cup of Espresso Romano brings a powerful and refreshing experience, walking in strength and grace brings a sense of peace and fulfillment.

Walking courageously with the Lord also means being intentional about cultivating both strength and grace in our lives. Just as making

Espresso Romano requires careful preparation and attention to detail, living in strength and grace requires us to be deliberate and mindful in our actions.

This involves making prayer and Bible study a regular part of our routine, attending church, and participating in fellowship with other believers. By making these practices a priority, we create space in our lives for God to work in us and to strengthen us.

Another important aspect of a courageous walk with the Lord is the willingness to trust in His strength and grace, even when it is challenging or difficult to understand. Just as the strength of espresso is complemented by the refreshing touch of lemon in Espresso Romano, the strength that comes from faith is often enhanced by the grace that God provides. This requires us to have faith that God knows what is best for us and to trust that He is leading us in the right direction. By placing our trust in God's strength and grace, we can navigate the challenges of life with confidence and peace, knowing that He is guiding our steps.

Walking courageously with the Lord also means being a source of strength and grace to others. Just as Espresso Romano provides a strong and refreshing experience, our faith and our relationship with God should provide encouragement and support to those around us. We can offer words of wisdom, share uplifting scriptures, and be a positive influence in the lives of others. By being a source of strength and grace, we reflect the love and grace of God and help others experience the power and compassion of a life lived in faith.

Living a life of courageous faith also means being open to the ways God wants to use us to strengthen and support others. Just as the process of making Espresso Romano involves transforming simple ingredients into a powerful drink, God can use our unique gifts and experiences to bring His strength and support to others. This involves being willing to share our stories, to use our gifts to serve others, and to be a vessel through which God's love and wisdom can flow. By being open to God's work in us and through us, we can make a positive impact on the lives of others and help them experience the strength and grace that comes from faith.

Walking courageously with the Lord also involves being grateful for the ways He strengthens and graces us. Just as each cup of Espresso Romano is a unique and special experience, each moment of God's strength and grace is a gift to be cherished. This involves cultivating an attitude of gratitude and taking time to thank God for His presence and His care. By being mindful of these moments, we can fully appreciate the depth of God's love and the peace that comes from knowing we are walking in His will.

In conclusion, walking courageously with the Lord is like enjoying a cup of Espresso Romano, strong with a hint of citrus, symbolizing strength with a touch of grace. It involves being strong in our faith, carrying a touch of grace with us, and trusting in God's strength and grace. By valuing the strength and grace that come from faith and making them a central part of our lives, we demonstrate our trust in God and our desire to live in His fullness. Remember, as John 1:16 tells us, "And of his fulness have all we received, and grace for grace." This verse is a powerful reminder of the fullness we find in Christ, much like the invigorating and refreshing experience of drinking Espresso Romano. So, let us take that courageous walk with the Lord, knowing that He is our strength and our guide, and let our lives be a testament to the strength and grace that come from faith. Just as a well-made Espresso Romano brings a strong and refreshing experience, our faithful walk with God can bring peace, joy, and inspiration to those around us, making our world a better and brighter place. By embracing the strength and grace of faith and relying on God's strength, we honor Him and reflect His love and grace in all that we do.

Chapter 26 Café Yaucono (Puerto Rico)

"For I am not ashamed of the gospel of Christ: for it is the power of God unto salvation to every one that believeth."

Romans 1:16

Ingredients:

- 1 cup water
- 1 tablespoon finely ground coffee (Yaucono brand, if available)
- Sugar (optional, to taste)

Equipment:

- Small saucepan
- Coffee filter or fine mesh sieve
- Small cups

Instructions:

1. In a small saucepan, bring the water to a boil.
2. Add the ground coffee and stir.
3. Remove from heat and let it steep for a few minutes.
4. Strain the coffee through a filter or sieve into small cups.
5. Add sugar to taste, if desired.
6. Serve hot.

Walking courageously with the Lord can be compared to savoring a cup of Café Yaucono, a bold and vibrant coffee from Puerto Rico that symbolizes the boldness of proclaiming the gospel. Café Yaucono is known for its rich and intense flavor, providing an invigorating experience with each sip. Similarly, our walk with the Lord should be marked by the boldness and confidence we have in sharing the gospel of Christ. The Bible tells us in Romans 1:16, "For I am not ashamed of the gospel of Christ: for it is the power of God unto salvation to every one that believeth." This verse reminds us of the transformative power of the gospel and the importance of proclaiming it with boldness and without shame, much like the bold flavor of Café Yaucono, offering a taste of God's love and power that is meant to be shared widely and confidently. Just as Café Yaucono is enjoyed for its strong and vibrant character, our faith should be vibrant and dynamic, impacting those around us and bringing the message of salvation to everyone we encounter.

Imagine starting your day with a cup of Café Yaucono. The process of making it involves brewing strong coffee that awakens your senses and energizes your spirit. In the same way, starting our day by reflecting on the boldness and power of the gospel can fill our hearts with courage and prepare us to share our faith with others. A man who walks courageously with the Lord finds strength in the gospel and lets that strength drive him to live boldly for Christ. This kind of faith is not only about maintaining personal devotion but also about actively and confidently sharing the good news with others, trusting in the power of the gospel to change lives.

Walking courageously with the Lord means being bold and vibrant in our faith, much like the intense flavor of Café Yaucono. Just as this coffee is appreciated for its strong and unapologetic character, our faith should be marked by a boldness that refuses to shy away from opportunities to share the gospel. This involves being unafraid to speak about our faith, to share our personal testimonies, and to engage in conversations about God's love and salvation. By being bold in our faith, we can make a significant impact on those around us, much like how a strong cup of coffee can invigorate and awaken the senses.

In our daily lives, there are numerous opportunities to be bold and vibrant in sharing the gospel. It could be through initiating conversations about faith with friends and family, participating in outreach activities, or using social media to share encouraging scriptures and testimonies. Each of these actions, when done with a heart full of faith and confidence, reflects the boldness of the gospel to those around us. Just as a well-made Café Yaucono brings a powerful and invigorating experience, our bold proclamation of the gospel can bring hope and transformation to the lives of others.

Walking courageously with the Lord also means embracing the boldness that comes from knowing the power of the gospel. Just as Café Yaucono is known for its robust flavor, the gospel is powerful and transformative, bringing salvation and new life to those who believe. This requires us to have confidence in the message we share, trusting that God's word will accomplish what He intends. By having this confidence, we can share the gospel boldly, knowing that it has the power to change hearts and lives.

Another important aspect of a courageous walk with the Lord is the willingness to stand firm in our beliefs, even when faced with opposition or ridicule. Just as Café Yaucono stands out for its strong and distinct flavor, our faith should stand out for its boldness and clarity. This involves being unapologetic about our faith, standing up for what we believe, and not allowing fear or doubt to silence our witness. By standing firm in our beliefs, we demonstrate the strength and conviction of our faith, much like the boldness of Café Yaucono.

Walking courageously with the Lord also means being a source of encouragement and inspiration to others. Just as Café Yaucono provides an invigorating experience, our faith should inspire and uplift those around us. We can offer words of encouragement, share uplifting scriptures, and support others in their faith journeys. By being a source of encouragement, we reflect the love and grace of God and help others experience the boldness and confidence that comes from knowing Him.

Living a life of courageous faith also means finding joy and fulfillment in sharing the gospel. Just as the enjoyment of Café Yaucono brings a sense of satisfaction, sharing the gospel brings a deep sense of joy and purpose. This involves recognizing the privilege and responsibility we have to share the good news and finding joy in the opportunities to do so. By embracing this joy, we can approach evangelism with enthusiasm and passion, making a positive impact on the lives of others.

Walking courageously with the Lord also involves being open to the guidance of the Holy Spirit as we share the gospel. Just as the process of making Café Yaucono requires attention and care, sharing the gospel requires us to be attentive to the leading of the Holy Spirit. This means being sensitive to opportunities to share our faith, listening for the Spirit's guidance in our conversations, and being obedient to His promptings. By being open to the Holy Spirit's guidance, we can share the gospel effectively and with confidence.

In conclusion, walking courageously with the Lord is like enjoying a cup of Café Yaucono, bold and vibrant, symbolizing the boldness required in sharing the gospel. It involves being bold and confident in our faith, trusting in the power of the gospel, and sharing it with others without shame. By valuing the boldness of the gospel and making it a central part of our lives, we demonstrate our commitment to God and our desire to proclaim His message of salvation. Remember, as Romans 1:16 tells us, "For I am not ashamed of the gospel of Christ: for it is the power of God unto salvation to every one that believeth." This verse is a powerful reminder of the transformative power of the gospel and the importance of sharing it boldly. So, let us take that courageous walk with the Lord, knowing that He is our strength and our guide, and let our lives be a testament to the boldness and power of the gospel. Just as a well-made Café Yaucono brings delight and energy, our bold and confident walk with God can bring hope, encouragement, and transformation to those around us, making our world a better and brighter place. By embracing the boldness of the gospel and sharing it with confidence, we honor God and reflect His love and grace in all that we do.

Chapter 27 Qishr (Yemen)

Have not I commanded thee? Be strong and of a good courage; be not afraid, neither be thou dismayed: for the Lord thy God is with thee whithersoever thou goest.

Joshua 1:9

Qishr is a traditional Yemeni coffee drink made from the husks of coffee cherries rather than the beans themselves. It has a unique flavor profile that includes spicy and slightly sweet notes.

Ingredients:

1. Coffee Husks: The dried outer husks of the coffee cherry, known as Qishr or cascara.

2. Ginger: Fresh or dried ginger, which adds a spicy, warming flavor.

3. Cinnamon: Ground or whole cinnamon sticks, providing a sweet and aromatic note.

4. Sugar: Typically used to sweeten the drink to taste.

Preparation

1. Boil Water: Bring water to a boil in a pot.

2. Add Ingredients: Add the coffee husks, ginger, cinnamon, and sugar to the boiling water.

3. Simmer: Let the mixture simmer for about 5-10 minutes.

4. Strain: Strain the mixture to remove the solids.

5. Serve: Pour the Qishr into cups and serve hot.

Qishr is a traditional Yemeni drink made from the husks of coffee cherries, rather than the beans. It has a unique flavor, with spicy and slightly sweet notes. To make Qishr, you need coffee husks, ginger, cinnamon, and sugar. The coffee husks are the dried outer parts of the coffee cherry, known as Qishr or cascara. Ginger adds a spicy, warming flavor, while cinnamon provides a sweet and aromatic note. Sugar is typically used to sweeten the drink to taste. To prepare Qishr, you start by boiling water in a pot. Once the water is boiling, you add the coffee husks, ginger, cinnamon, and sugar. Let the mixture simmer for about 5-10 minutes, then strain it to remove the solids. Finally, pour the Qishr into cups and serve it hot. This drink is traditionally served in small cups and is known for its invigorating and refreshing qualities. It is a popular beverage in Yemen, especially during social gatherings and ceremonies. The use of coffee husks makes Qishr a more sustainable option, as it uses parts of the coffee plant that are often discarded. This drink can be compared to the boldness needed in the life of a Christian. Just as Qishr stands out with its unique flavors, Christians are called to stand out in their faith and live boldly for Christ. In Joshua 1:9, the Bible says, "Have not I commanded thee? Be strong and of a good courage; be not afraid, neither be thou dismayed: for the LORD thy God is with thee whithersoever thou goest." This verse encourages Christians to be bold and courageous, knowing that God is always with them. Similarly, 2 Timothy 1:7 says, "For God hath not given us the spirit of fear; but of power, and of love, and of a sound mind." This verse reminds Christians that God gives them the power to overcome fear and live boldly. In Ephesians 6:10, it says, "Finally, my brethren, be strong in the Lord, and in the power of his might." Christians are called to be strong in the Lord and rely on His power. Just as Qishr is made from parts of the coffee plant that are often overlooked, God often uses people and things that the world overlooks to accomplish His purposes. In 1 Corinthians 1:27, it says, "But God hath chosen the foolish things of the world to confound the wise; and God hath chosen the weak things of the world to confound the things which are mighty." This verse shows that God can use anyone, no matter how insignificant they may seem, to do great things. In Hebrews 4:16, it says, "Let us therefore come boldly unto the throne of grace, that we may obtain mercy, and find grace to help in time of need." This verse encourages Christians to come boldly to God in prayer, knowing that they can receive His mercy and grace. In Acts 4:29, the early Christians prayed for boldness, saying, "And now, Lord, behold their threatenings: and grant unto thy servants, that with all boldness they may speak thy word." This prayer shows the importance of boldness in sharing the gospel. Just as Qishr has a unique and bold flavor, Christians are called to live with a unique and bold faith. In Philippians 1:20, Paul says, "According to my earnest expectation and my hope, that in nothing I shall be ashamed, but that with all boldness, as always, so now also Christ shall be magnified in my body, whether it be by life, or by death." Paul's words remind Christians to live boldly for Christ, magnifying Him in everything they do. In Proverbs 28:1, it says, "The wicked flee when no man pursueth: but the righteous are bold as a lion." This verse shows that the righteous, those who live according to God's ways, can have boldness and confidence. In 1 John 4:17, it says, "Herein is our love made perfect, that we may have boldness in the day of judgment: because as he is, so are we in this world." This verse reminds Christians that their love is made perfect in Christ, giving them boldness. Just as Qishr stands out with its unique ingredients and preparation, Christians are called to stand out with their unique faith and boldness. In Matthew 5:14-16, Jesus says, "Ye are the light of the world. A city that is set on a hill cannot be hid. Neither do men light a candle, and put it under a bushel, but on a candlestick; and it giveth light unto all that are in the house. Let your light so shine before men, that they may see your good works, and glorify your Father which is in heaven." These verses call Christians to let their light shine brightly, showing the world the love and truth of Christ. In Romans 1:16, Paul says, "For I am not ashamed of the gospel of Christ: for it is the power of God unto salvation to every one that believeth; to the Jew first, and also to the Greek." This verse encourages Christians to be unashamed and bold in sharing the gospel. In Hebrews 13:6, it says, "So that we may boldly say, The Lord is my helper, and I will not fear what man shall do unto me." This verse reminds Christians that they can have boldness and confidence because the Lord is their helper. In 2 Corinthians 3:12, it says, "Seeing then that we have such hope, we use great plainness of speech." This verse encourages Christians to speak boldly and plainly about their hope in Christ. Just as Qishr has a distinct and bold flavor, Christians are called to have a distinct and bold faith. In Mark 16:15, Jesus says, "Go ye into all the world, and preach the gospel to every creature." This command calls Christians to be bold in sharing the gospel with everyone. In Ephesians 3:12, it says, "In whom we have boldness and access with confidence by the faith of him." This verse reminds Christians that through faith in Christ, they have boldness and confidence. In Psalm 138:3, it says, "In the day when I cried thou answeredst me, and strengthenedst me with strength in my soul." This verse shows that God strengthens His people, giving them the boldness they need. In Colossians 4:6, it says, "Let your speech be always with grace, seasoned with salt, that ye may know how ye ought to answer every man." This verse encourages Christians to speak with grace and boldness, knowing how to answer everyone. In Acts 28:31, it says, "Preaching the kingdom of God, and teaching those things which concern the Lord Jesus Christ, with all confidence, no man forbidding him." This verse shows the boldness of the early Christians in preaching and teaching about Jesus. In Proverbs 3:5-6, it says, "Trust in the LORD with all thine heart; and lean not unto thine own understanding. In all thy ways acknowledge him, and he shall direct thy paths." These verses remind Christians to trust in the Lord and be bold in their faith, knowing that He will guide them. In John 14:27, Jesus says, "Peace I leave with you, my peace I give unto you: not as the world giveth, give I unto you. Let not your heart be troubled, neither let it be afraid." This verse encourages Christians to have peace and boldness, knowing that Jesus gives them His peace. In 1 Corinthians 16:13, it says, "Watch ye, stand fast in the faith, quit you like men, be strong." This verse calls Christians to be strong and bold in their faith. In Isaiah 41:10, it says, "Fear thou not; for I am with thee: be not dismayed; for I am thy God: I will strengthen thee; yea, I will help thee; yea, I will uphold thee with the right hand of my righteousness." This verse reminds Christians that God is with them, giving them the strength and boldness they need. In Psalm 27:1, it says, "The LORD is my light and my salvation; whom shall I fear? the LORD is the strength of my life; of whom shall I be afraid?" This verse shows that with the Lord as their light and salvation, Christians have no reason to fear. In Philippians 4:13, it says, "I can do all things through Christ which strengtheneth me." This verse reminds Christians that they can do all things through Christ, who gives them strength and boldness. In Matthew 10:16, Jesus says, "Behold, I send you forth as sheep in the midst of wolves: be ye therefore wise as serpents, and harmless as doves." This verse calls Christians to be wise and bold in their faith, even in difficult situations. In Hebrews 13:5, it says, "Let your conversation be without covetousness; and be content with such things as ye have: for he hath said, I will never leave thee, nor forsake thee." This verse reminds Christians that God is always with them, giving them the boldness and confidence they need. In 2 Timothy 2:15, it says, "Study to shew thyself approved unto God, a workman that needeth not to be ashamed, rightly dividing the word of truth." This verse encourages Christians to be diligent and bold in studying and sharing the word of truth. In Psalm 23:4, it says, "Yea, though I walk through the valley of the shadow of death, I will fear no evil: for thou art with me; thy rod and thy staff they comfort me." This verse shows that even in the darkest times, Christians can have boldness and confidence because God is with them. In James 1:12, it says, "Blessed is the man that endureth temptation: for when he is tried, he shall receive the crown of life, which the Lord hath promised to them that love him." This verse reminds Christians that enduring trials with boldness will lead to a reward. In 1 Peter 3:15, it says, "But sanctify the Lord God in your hearts: and be ready always to give an answer to every man that asketh you a reason of the hope that is in you with meekness and fear."

This verse encourages Christians to be ready to share their hope with boldness and humility. In Romans 8:31, it says, "What shall we then say to these things? If God be for us, who can be against us?" This verse shows that with God on their side, Christians can be bold and confident. In Matthew 28:18-20, Jesus says, "All power is given unto me in heaven and in earth. Go ye therefore, and teach all nations, baptizing them in the name of the Father, and of the Son, and of the Holy Ghost: Teaching them to observe all things whatsoever I have commanded you: and, lo, I am with you alway, even unto the end of the world." These verses call Christians to be bold in making disciples of all nations, knowing that Jesus is always with them. In John 16:33, Jesus says, "These things I have spoken unto you, that in me ye might have peace. In the world ye shall have tribulation: but be of good cheer; I have overcome the world." This verse encourages Christians to have peace and boldness, knowing that Jesus has overcome the world. In Psalm 118:6, it says, "The LORD is on my side; I will not fear: what can man do unto me?" This verse shows that with the Lord on their side, Christians have no reason to fear and can live boldly. In Isaiah 54:17, it says, "No weapon that is formed against thee shall prosper; and every tongue that shall rise against thee in judgment thou shalt condemn. This is the heritage of the servants of the LORD, and their righteousness is of me, saith the LORD." This verse reminds Christians that God will protect them, giving them the boldness they need to face any challenge. Just as Qishr stands out with its unique and bold flavor, Christians are called to live with a unique and bold faith, shining their light for the world to see.

Chapter 28 Café Crema (Switzerland)

"And thine ears shall hear a word behind thee, saying, This is the way, walk ye in it, when ye turn to the right hand, and when ye turn to the left." Isaiah 30:21

Ingredients:

- 1 shot (1.5 oz) espresso
- 1 cup steamed milk

Equipment:

- Espresso machine
- Milk steamer
- Mug

Instructions:

1. Brew a shot of espresso.
2. Steam the milk until it is hot and frothy.
3. Pour the espresso into a mug.
4. Add the steamed milk and stir.
5. Serve immediately.

Walking courageously with the Lord can be compared to savoring a cup of Café Crema, a smooth and creamy Swiss coffee that symbolizes the smooth path of righteousness. Café Crema is known for its velvety texture and rich flavor, providing a comforting and satisfying experience with each sip. Similarly, our walk with the Lord should be marked by the smoothness and clarity of the path of righteousness that He lays out for us. The Bible tells us in Isaiah 30:21, "And thine ears shall hear a word behind thee, saying, This is the way, walk ye in it, when ye turn to the right hand, and when ye turn to the left." This verse reminds us of the guidance that God provides, directing our steps and showing us the way to walk in righteousness, much like the creamy and smooth experience of drinking Café Crema offers a taste of the clear and comforting direction that God provides in our lives.

Imagine starting your day with a cup of Café Crema. The process of making it involves brewing strong coffee and adding just the right amount of milk or cream, resulting in a drink that is both rich and smooth. In the same way, starting our day by seeking God's guidance and reflecting on His righteousness can fill our hearts with peace and clarity, preparing us to navigate the day with confidence and assurance. A man who walks courageously with the Lord finds peace in the knowledge that God is guiding his steps and providing a smooth path for him to follow. This kind of faith is not only about avoiding pitfalls but also about walking confidently in the direction that God has set, much like enjoying the smooth, creamy texture of Café Crema.

Walking courageously with the Lord means embracing the smooth path of righteousness that He provides. Just as Café Crema is a blend of strong coffee and creamy milk that creates a smooth and satisfying experience, our relationship with Christ involves following His guidance and walking in the path of righteousness that He has set before us. This requires us to be attentive to God's voice, to listen for His direction, and to follow His leading, even when the way ahead is not entirely clear. By doing so, we can experience the peace and clarity that comes from walking in God's will, much like the satisfying experience of drinking a well-made Café Crema.

In our daily lives, there are many opportunities to walk in the path of righteousness and to seek God's guidance. It could be through moments of prayer, studying the Bible, or seeking counsel from wise and trusted mentors. Each of these actions, when done with a heart open to God's leading, helps to strengthen our relationship with Him and to ensure that we are walking in the direction that He has set for us. Just as a cup of Café Crema brings comfort and satisfaction, walking in God's path brings a sense of peace and fulfillment.

Walking courageously with the Lord also means being intentional about following His guidance and walking in His ways. Just as making Café Crema requires careful preparation and attention to detail, walking in the path of righteousness requires us to be deliberate and mindful in our actions. This involves making prayer and Bible study a regular part of our routine, attending church, and participating in fellowship with other believers. By making these practices a priority, we create space in our lives for God to guide us and to show us the way to walk in righteousness.

Another important aspect of a courageous walk with the Lord is the willingness to trust in His direction, even when it is challenging or difficult to understand. Just as the smooth and creamy texture of Café Crema is achieved through a careful blending process, the smooth path of righteousness is often achieved through trusting God's process and His timing. This requires us to have faith that God knows what is best for us and to trust that He is leading us in the right direction. By placing our trust in God, we can navigate the challenges of life with confidence and peace, knowing that He is guiding our steps.

Walking courageously with the Lord also means being a source of guidance and encouragement to others. Just as Café Crema provides a comforting and satisfying experience, our faith and our relationship with God should provide encouragement and support to those around us. We can offer words of wisdom, share uplifting scriptures, and be a positive influence in the lives of others. By being a source of guidance and encouragement, we reflect the love and grace of God and help others experience the smooth path of righteousness.

Living a life of courageous faith also means being open to the ways God wants to use us to guide and support others. Just as the process of making Café Crema involves transforming simple ingredients into a delightful drink, God can use our unique gifts and experiences to bring

His guidance and support to others. This involves being willing to share our stories, to use our gifts to serve others, and to be a vessel through which God's love and wisdom can flow. By being open to God's work in us and through us, we can make a positive impact on the lives of others and help them experience the smooth path of righteousness.

Walking courageously with the Lord also involves being grateful for the guidance and direction He provides. Just as each cup of Café Crema is a unique and special experience, each moment of God's guidance is a gift to be cherished. This involves cultivating an attitude of gratitude and taking time to thank God for His presence and His care. By being mindful of these moments, we can fully appreciate the depth of God's love and the peace that comes from knowing we are walking in His will.

In conclusion, walking courageously with the Lord is like enjoying a cup of Café Crema, smooth and creamy, symbolizing the smooth path of righteousness that God provides. It involves walking in the path of righteousness, seeking His guidance intentionally, and sharing His love and wisdom with others. By valuing the smooth path of righteousness and making it a central part of our lives, we demonstrate our trust in God and our desire to live in His will. Remember, as Isaiah 30:21 tells us, "And thine ears shall hear a word behind thee, saying, This is the way, walk ye in it, when ye turn to the right hand, and when ye turn to the left." This verse is a powerful reminder of the guidance that God provides, much like the comforting and satisfying experience of drinking a Café Crema. So, let us take that courageous walk with the Lord, knowing that He is our strength and our guide, and let our lives be a testament to the smooth path of righteousness that He provides. Just as a wellmade Café Crema brings comfort and satisfaction, our faithful walk with God can bring peace, joy, and inspiration to those around us, making our world a better and brighter place. By embracing the smooth path of righteousness and sharing it with confidence, we honor God and reflect His love and grace in all that we do.

Chapter 29 Café Cortado (Spain)

"But the fruit of the Spirit is love, joy, peace, longsuffering, gentleness, goodness, faith." Galatians 5:22

Ingredients:

- 1 shot (1.5 oz)

espresso

- 1-2 tablespoons warm milk

Equipment:

- Espresso machine
- Milk steamer or saucepan
- Cup

Instructions:

1. Brew a shot of espresso.
2. Warm the milk in a steamer or saucepan.
3. Add the warm milk to the espresso.
4. Serve immediately.

Walking courageously with the Lord can be compared to savoring a cup of Café Cortado, a Spanish coffee that is strong with a touch of milk, symbolizing strength with gentleness. Café Cortado is known for its bold espresso flavor balanced by a small amount of warm milk, creating a drink that is both intense and smooth. Similarly, our walk with the Lord should be marked by a strong and unwavering faith that is always accompanied by gentleness. The Bible tells us in Galatians 5:22, "But the fruit of the Spirit is love, joy, peace, longsuffering, gentleness, goodness, faith." This verse reminds us that true strength in our faith should be tempered with gentleness and the other fruits of the Spirit, much like the bold flavor of espresso complemented by the smooth touch of milk in Café Cortado, offering a taste of the powerful yet gentle faith we are called to embody in our lives.

Imagine starting your day with a cup of Café Cortado. The process of making it involves brewing a strong shot of espresso and adding a small amount of milk, resulting in a drink that is both bold and comforting. In the same way, starting our day by seeking God's strength and reflecting on His gentleness can fill our hearts with His presence and prepare us to face the day with courage and compassion. A man who walks courageously with the Lord finds strength in his faith and lets that strength be tempered with gentleness. This kind of faith is not only about standing firm in the face of adversity but also about extending kindness and understanding to others, much like savoring the strong yet smooth taste of Café Cortado.

Walking courageously with the Lord means embracing the strength that comes from faith while also carrying a touch of gentleness with us. Just as Café Cortado is a blend of strong espresso and the gentle addition of milk, our relationship with Christ involves being strong in our convictions and actions, while also being gracious and compassionate. This requires us to be firm in our beliefs, to stand up for what is right, and to persevere through trials, while also showing love, forgiveness, and understanding to those around us. By doing so, we can experience the fullness of Christ, much like the invigorating experience of drinking a well-made Café Cortado.

In our daily lives, there are many opportunities to practice being strong in our faith and carrying a touch of gentleness. It could be through standing up for someone who is being treated unfairly, offering forgiveness to someone who has wronged us, or showing kindness to a stranger. Each of these actions, when done with a heart full of faith and gentleness, reflects the strength and compassion of Christ. Just as a cup of Café Cortado brings a powerful and comforting experience, walking in strength and gentleness brings a sense of peace and fulfillment.

Walking courageously with the Lord also means being intentional about cultivating both strength and gentleness in our lives. Just as making Café Cortado requires careful preparation and attention to detail, living in strength and gentleness requires us to be deliberate and mindful in our actions. This involves making prayer and Bible study a regular part of our routine, attending church, and participating in fellowship with other believers. By making these practices a priority, we create space in our lives for God to work in us and to strengthen us.

Another important aspect of a courageous walk with the Lord is the willingness to trust in His strength and gentleness, even when it is challenging or difficult to understand. Just as the strength of espresso is complemented by the gentle touch of milk in Café Cortado, the strength that comes from faith is often enhanced by the gentleness that God provides. This requires us to have faith that God knows what is best for us and to trust that He is leading us in the right direction. By placing our trust in God's strength and gentleness, we can navigate the challenges of life with confidence and peace, knowing that He is guiding our steps.

Walking courageously with the Lord also means being a source of strength and gentleness to others. Just as Café Cortado provides a strong and comforting experience, our faith and our relationship with God should provide encouragement and support to those around us. We can offer words of wisdom, share uplifting scriptures, and be a positive influence in the lives of others. By being a source of strength and gentleness, we reflect the love and grace of God and help others experience the power and compassion of a life lived in faith.

Living a life of courageous faith also means being open to the ways God wants to use us to strengthen and support others. Just as the process of making Café Cortado involves transforming simple ingredients into a powerful drink, God can use our unique gifts and experiences to bring His strength and support to others. This involves being willing to share our stories, to use our gifts to serve others, and to be a vessel through which God's love and wisdom can flow. By being open to God's work in us and through us, we can make a positive impact on the lives of others and help them experience the strength and gentleness that comes from faith.

Walking courageously with the Lord also involves being grateful for the ways He strengthens and graces us. Just as each cup of Café Cortado is a unique and special experience, each moment of God's strength and gentleness is a gift to be cherished. This involves cultivating an attitude of gratitude and taking time to thank God for His presence and His care. By being mindful of these moments, we can fully appreciate the depth of God's love and the peace that comes from knowing we are walking in His will.

In conclusion, walking courageously with the Lord is like enjoying a cup of Café Cortado, strong with a touch of milk, symbolizing strength with gentleness. It involves being strong in our faith, carrying a touch of gentleness with us, and trusting in God's strength and gentleness. By valuing the strength and gentleness that come from faith and making them a central part of our lives, we demonstrate our trust in God and our desire to live in His fullness. Remember, as Galatians 5:22 tells us, "But the fruit of the Spirit is love, joy, peace, longsuffering, gentleness, goodness, faith." This verse is a powerful reminder of the fruits of the Spirit that we should embody, much like the invigorating and comforting experience of drinking Café Cortado. So, let us take that courageous walk with the Lord, knowing that He is our strength and our guide, and let our lives be a testament to the strength and gentleness that come from faith. Just as a wellmade Café Cortado brings a powerful and comforting experience, our faithful walk with God can bring peace, joy, and inspiration to those around us, making our world a better and brighter place. By embracing the strength and gentleness of faith and relying on God's strength, we honor Him and reflect His love and grace in all that we do.

Chapter 30 Egg Coffee (Vietnam)

For my thoughts are not your thoughts, neither are your ways my ways, saith the Lord." Isaiah 55:8

Ingredients:

- 2 egg yolks
- 2 tablespoons sugar
- 2 tablespoons sweetened condensed milk
- 1/2 cup (120ml) strong black coffee (hot)

Instructions:
1.Prepare the Coffee:

- Brew a strong cup of black coffee. You can use a drip coffee maker, a French press, or any method that produces strong coffee. Vietnamese coffee or espresso works best for this recipe.

- Once brewed, keep the coffee hot and set it aside.

2. Separate the Eggs:

- Separate the egg yolks from the whites. You only need the yolks for this recipe. Save the whites for another use if desired.

3. Whip the Egg Yolks:

- Place the egg yolks in a mixing bowl.

- Add 2 tablespoons of sugar to the yolks.

- Using a hand mixer or a whisk, beat the yolks and sugar together until the mixture becomes thick, creamy, and pale in color. This should take about 3-5 minutes with a hand mixer, or longer if whisking by hand.

4. Add the Condensed Milk:

- Once the yolks and sugar are well mixed, add 2 tablespoons of sweetened condensed milk.

- Continue to beat the mixture until it is fully incorporated and becomes light and fluffy. The consistency should be smooth and creamy.

5. Combine the Coffee and Egg Mixture:

- Pour the hot, strong black coffee into a serving cup or mug.

- Gently spoon the whipped egg mixture on top of the coffee. The egg mixture should float on top, creating a layered effect.

- Optionally, you can use a spoon to slightly mix the egg cream into the coffee for a blended texture, or leave it layered for a traditional presentation.

6. Serve:
- Serve the Egg Coffee immediately while it is still hot.

Walking courageously with the Lord can be compared to savoring a cup of Egg Coffee from Vietnam, an unexpected combination that symbolizes the surprising ways God works in our lives. Egg Coffee is made by whisking egg yolks with sugar and sweetened condensed milk until fluffy and then pouring this creamy mixture over hot black coffee, creating a drink that is both rich and unexpectedly delightful. Similarly, our walk with the Lord should be marked by an openness to the surprising and unexpected ways God answers our prayers and guides our paths. The Bible tells us in Isaiah 55:8, "For my thoughts are not your thoughts, neither are your ways my ways, saith the Lord." This verse reminds us that God's ways and thoughts are higher than ours, much like the unique combination of egg and coffee offers a taste of the remarkable and surprising work of God in our lives.

Imagine starting your day with a cup of Egg Coffee. The process of making it involves whisking egg yolks with sugar and condensed milk until they become fluffy and then adding this mixture to strong black coffee, resulting in a drink that is both creamy and rich. In the same way, starting our day by reflecting on the surprising and unexpected ways God works can fill our hearts with wonder and prepare us to face the day with an open and trusting spirit. A man who walks courageously with the Lord finds joy in the surprises that God brings into his life and lets those surprises strengthen his faith. This kind of faith is not only about enduring the expected challenges but also about celebrating the unexpected blessings and answers to prayers, much like savoring the unique and delightful taste of Egg Coffee.

Walking courageously with the Lord means being open to the unexpected ways God works in our lives. Just as Egg Coffee is an unexpected combination that creates a delightful experience, our relationship with Christ involves experiencing His work in ways that we might not anticipate. This requires us to be flexible and open-minded, to trust that God knows what is best for us, and to embrace the surprising answers to our prayers. By doing so, we can experience the fullness of God's work in our lives, much like the satisfying experience of drinking a well-made Egg Coffee.

In our daily lives, there are many opportunities to see and appreciate the surprising ways God answers our prayers. It could be through unexpected blessings, new opportunities, or even challenges that lead to growth. Each of these experiences, when viewed with a heart full of faith and openness, reflects the surprising and wonderful work of God. Just as a cup of Egg Coffee brings a rich and unexpected experience, walking in openness to God's surprising ways brings a sense of wonder and fulfillment.

Walking courageously with the Lord also means being intentional about seeking and recognizing the surprising ways God works. Just as making Egg Coffee requires careful preparation and attention to detail, being open to God's unexpected work requires us to be deliberate and mindful in our actions. This involves making prayer and reflection a regular part of our routine, being attentive to the ways God might be speaking to us, and being willing to follow His lead even when it is unexpected. By making these practices a priority, we create space in our lives for God to surprise us and to work in wonderful ways.

Another important aspect of a courageous walk with the Lord is the willingness to trust in His ways, even when they are surprising or difficult to understand. Just as the unique combination of egg and coffee in Egg Coffee creates a delightful drink, the surprising ways God works often lead to outcomes that are far better than we could have imagined. This requires us to have faith that God's ways are higher than ours and to trust that He is leading us in the right direction. By placing our trust in God's surprising ways, we can navigate the challenges of life with confidence and peace, knowing that He is guiding our steps.

Walking courageously with the Lord also means being a source of encouragement and inspiration to others through the surprising ways God works in our lives. Just as Egg Coffee provides a unique and delightful experience, our faith and our relationship with God should provide encouragement and support to those around us. We can share our testimonies of how God has worked in unexpected ways, offer words of encouragement, and be a positive influence in the lives of others. By being a source of encouragement through the surprising ways God works, we reflect His love and grace and help others experience the wonder of His work.

Living a life of courageous faith also means being open to the ways God wants to use us to bring surprising blessings to others. Just as the process of making Egg Coffee involves transforming simple ingredients into a delightful drink, God can use our unique gifts and experiences to bring His blessings to others in unexpected ways. This involves being willing to share our stories, to use our gifts to serve others, and to be a vessel through which God's surprising work can flow. By being open to God's work in us and through us, we can make a positive impact on the lives of others and help them experience the surprising and wonderful work of God.

Walking courageously with the Lord also involves being grateful for the surprising ways He works in our lives. Just as each cup of Egg Coffee is a unique and special experience, each moment of God's surprising work is a gift to be cherished. This involves cultivating an attitude of gratitude and taking time to thank God for His presence and His care. By being mindful of these moments, we can fully appreciate the depth of God's love and the joy that comes from knowing we are walking in His ways.

In conclusion, walking courageously with the Lord is like enjoying a cup of Egg Coffee, an unexpected combination that symbolizes the surprising ways God works. It involves being open to the unexpected ways God answers prayers, seeking His guidance intentionally, and sharing His love and surprises with others. By valuing the surprising ways God works and making them a central part of our lives, we demonstrate our trust in Him and our desire to live in His fullness. Remember, as Isaiah 55:8 tells us, "For my thoughts are not your thoughts, neither are your ways my ways, saith the Lord." This verse is a powerful reminder of the higher and unexpected ways God works, much like the unique and delightful experience of drinking Egg Coffee. So, let us take that courageous walk with the Lord, knowing that He is our strength and our guide, and let our lives be a testament to the surprising and wonderful ways God works. Just as a wellmade Egg Coffee brings a rich and delightful experience, our faithful walk with God can bring joy, wonder, and inspiration to those around us, making our world a better and brighter place. By embracing the surprising ways God works and relying on His guidance, we honor Him and reflect His love and grace in all that we do.

Don't miss out!

Visit the website below and you can sign up to receive emails whenever Joshua Rhoades publishes a new book. There's no charge and no obligation.

https://books2read.com/r/B-A-AJLBB-VMXWD

BOOKS 2 READ

Connecting independent readers to independent writers.

Did you love *30 Day Devotional - Bold and Strong- Coffee Devotions for a Courageous Christian Walk*? Then you should read *Authentic Christianity: The Heart of Old Time Religion*[1] by Joshua Rhoades!

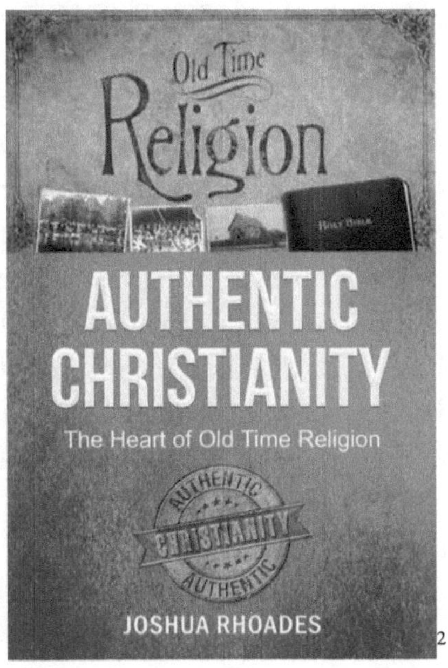

"Authentic Christianity - The Heart of Old Time Religion" is a book that calls readers back to the simple, yet profound, idea of believing and behaving according to Scripture. The author emphasizes it's about having a sincere faith in God and living out that faith in everyday life based on what the Bible teaches. This book breaks down the idea that authentic Christianity is rooted in simply believing in the truths of the Bible and letting those beliefs shape how you live. It reminds readers that the Bible is the ultimate guide for how to live a life that pleases God, and it encourages them to read and study Scripture regularly to understand what God wants from His followers. The book stresses

---

1. https://books2read.com/u/bMDq07

2. https://books2read.com/u/bMDq07

that believing is more than just saying you have faith; it's about truly trusting in God's Word and allowing it to influence your thoughts, actions, and decisions. Behaving Biblically means living out the principles found in the Bible. The author makes it clear that these actions are not about earning God's favor but are a natural response to the love and grace that God has already shown through Jesus Christ. The book also points out that living a Biblical life can be challenging in today's world, where many people have different values, but it encourages readers to stand firm in their faith and let the Bible be their guide, no matter what. It reassures readers that they don't have to do this on their own, as God provides strength and guidance through the Holy Spirit. "Authentic Christianity - The Heart of Old Time Religion" is a powerful reminder that true Christianity is not complicated; it's about believing what the Bible says and letting that belief guide how you live every day. The book encourages readers to get back to the basics of their faith, to trust in God's Word, and to live in a way that reflects the teachings of the Lord JesusChrist. It's a book that will inspire and challenge you to live out your faith in a real and meaningful way, not just in church on Sundays, but in every aspect of your life. Whether you're a new believer or someone who has been a Christian for a long time, this book will help you deepen your faith and remind you of the importance of simply believing and behaving Biblically according to Scripture. It's a call to return to the heart of Christianity, where faith is genuine, and actions speak louder than words, making it a valuable resource for anyone who wants to live a life that truly honors God.